Zen and the Art of Sarcasm. A Stress Relief and Funny Adult

Mindfulness Meets Snark in This Hilariously Relatable Anti-Stress

Snark & Scribbles: Coloring Outside the Lines of Adulthood

Book 1

Lola Laughton

Why Adult Coloring is the Secret to Relaxation and Joy: A Splash of Color, a Dash of Humor

In a world dominated by digital screens, endless notifications, and constant to-do lists, the idea of sitting down with a box of colored pencils and a coloring book might sound quaint. But this "childhood pastime" has found a resurgence among adults, and for good reason. Adult coloring books aren't just about filling shapes with color; they're a form of self-care, relaxation, and even a way to spark joy—especially when combined with a dose of humor.

Let's explore why adult coloring is more than just a fleeting trend and how combining it with funny quotes adds a whole new layer of therapeutic value.

The Magic of Adult Coloring: More Than Staying Inside the Lines Adult coloring has been touted as a mindfulness activity, akin to meditation.

Here's why it works:
   1 Stress Relief: When you focus on filling intricate patterns with colors, your mind lets go of intrusive thoughts. The repetitive motion has a calming effect on the brain, similar to the soothing nature of knitting or yoga.
   2 Creativity Boost: In a world where adult responsibilities can stifle creativity, coloring invites you to experiment with shades, textures, and styles. It's like giving your inner child permission to play.
   3 Improved Focus: Coloring requires a certain level of concentration. This engagement can help train your brain to focus better in other aspects of life.
   4 A Screen-Free Zone: Stepping away from screens to do something tactile can help reset your mind and improve overall well-being.

Why Add Funny Quotes? The Science of Laughter Meets Creativity

While coloring soothes the mind, adding funny quotes to the mix can elevate the experience to pure joy. Here's why humor is a perfect pairing:

1 Instant Mood Boost: Laughter triggers the release of endorphins, your body's natural feel-good chemicals. Pairing a witty one-liner with coloring makes it impossible not to crack a smile.

2 Perspective Shift: Humor has a way of reframing situations. A coloring page adorned with a quote like, "I'm not arguing, I'm just explaining why I'm right," brings a lighthearted lens to life's absurdities.

3 Keeps Things Fun: Coloring intricate mandalas or abstract patterns can sometimes feel a bit too serious. Funny quotes act as a reminder that this is about fun, not perfection.

4 A Conversation Starter: If you're coloring with friends or family, humorous quotes can spark laughter and connection, making the experience even more enriching.

How to Get Started: Combining Coloring and Comedy

Ready to dive in? Here are some tips to get the most out of your colorful and comedic journey:

1 Choose the Right Coloring Book: Look for books that blend intricate designs with cheeky quotes. Whether it's sass-filled affirmations or workplace humor, pick what resonates with you.

2 Set the Mood: Gather your supplies—markers, colored pencils, or even gel pens—and set up a cozy spot with good lighting. Bonus points for a cup of tea or glass of wine.

3 Share the Joy: Invite friends over for a "color and comedy" night. Everyone can pick a page, color, and read out loud their chosen quote for a communal laugh.

4 Display Your Masterpieces: Once you've finished a page, display it somewhere visible—like your fridge or workspace—to remind you of the lighter side of life.

Why This Combo is a Self-Care Essential

Incorporating funny quotes into adult coloring isn't just about laughter; it's about finding balance. Life can be serious, demanding, and chaotic. But when you sit down to color a snarky, rainbow-colored cactus alongside the words, "Can't touch this," you're giving yourself permission to take a break and embrace joy.

Adult coloring, infused with humor, offers a delightful antidote to the pressures of adulthood. It's a simple yet powerful way to reconnect with creativity, laughter, and yourself. So, grab those colored pencils and start filling your world with hues and humor—you deserve it.

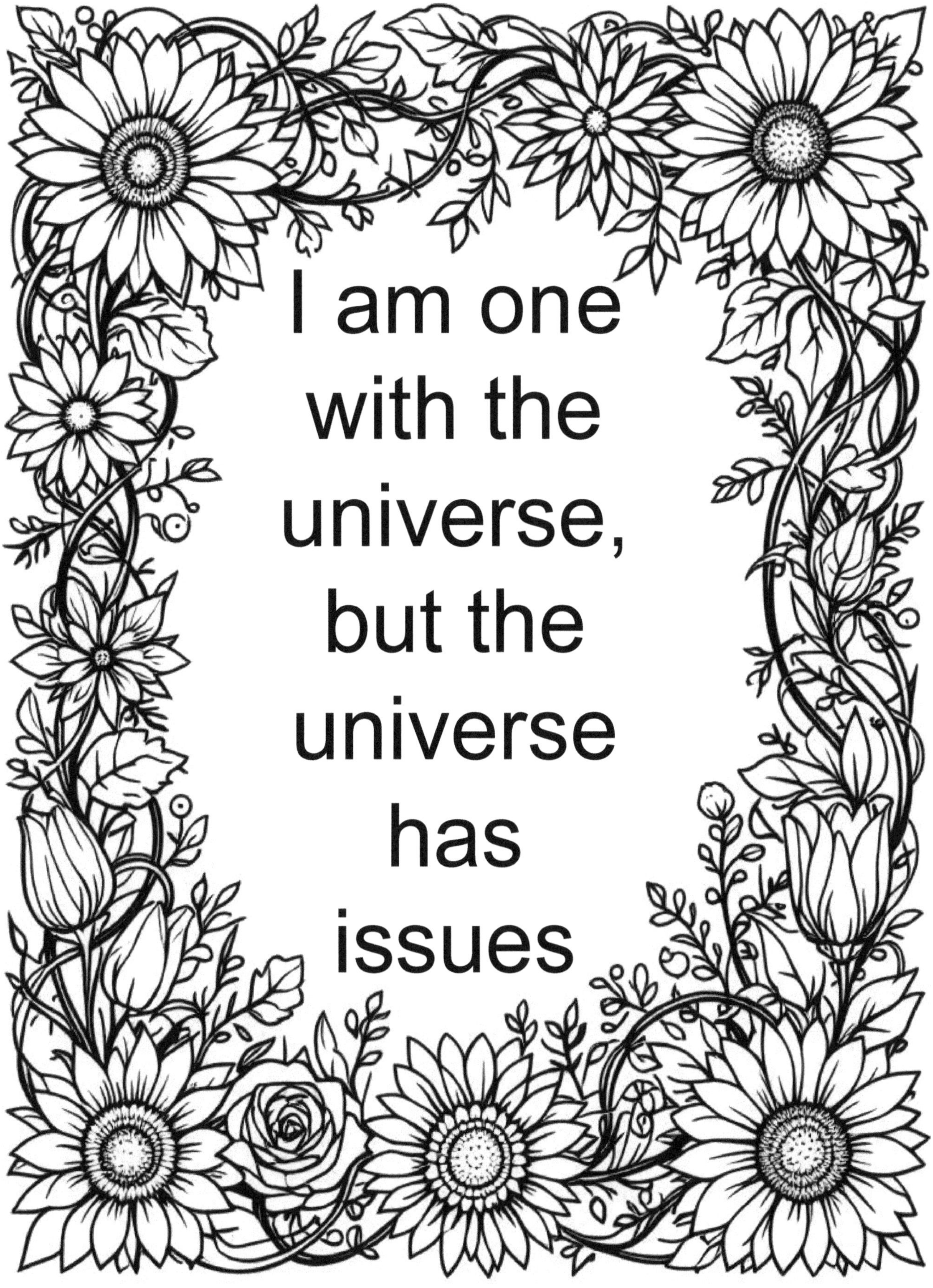
I am one with the universe, but the universe has issues

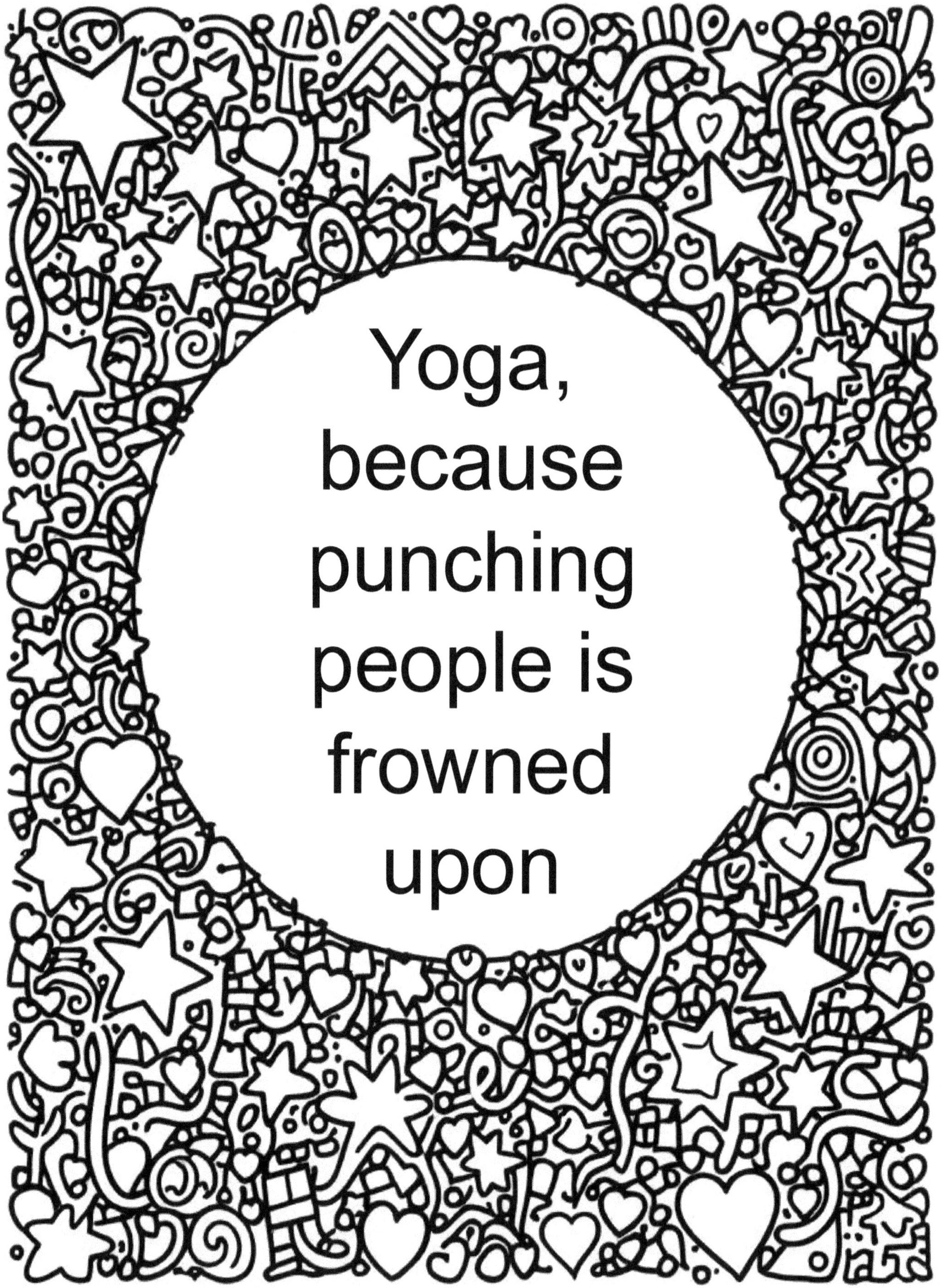
Yoga,
because
punching
people is
frowned
upon

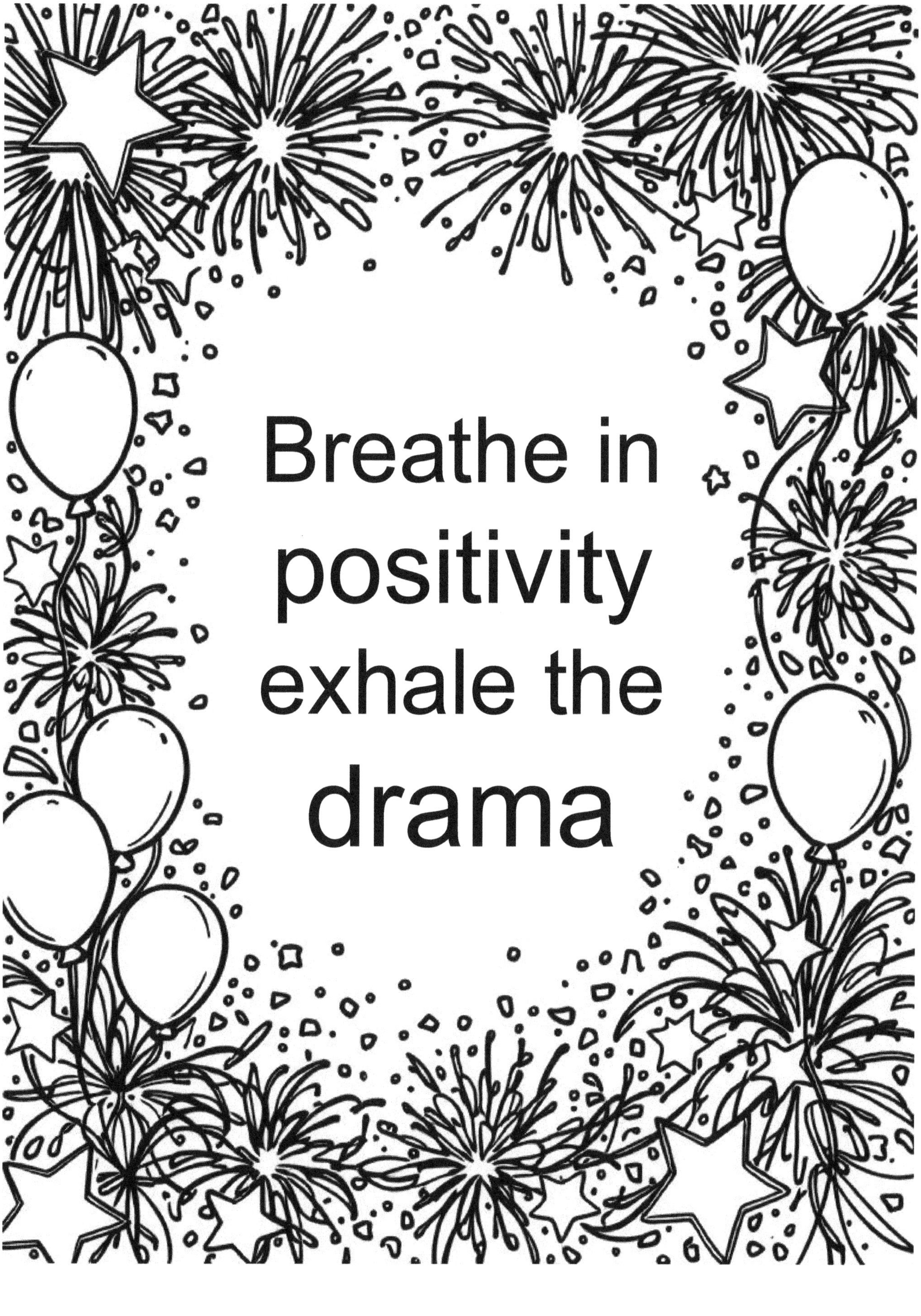
Breathe in positivity exhale the drama

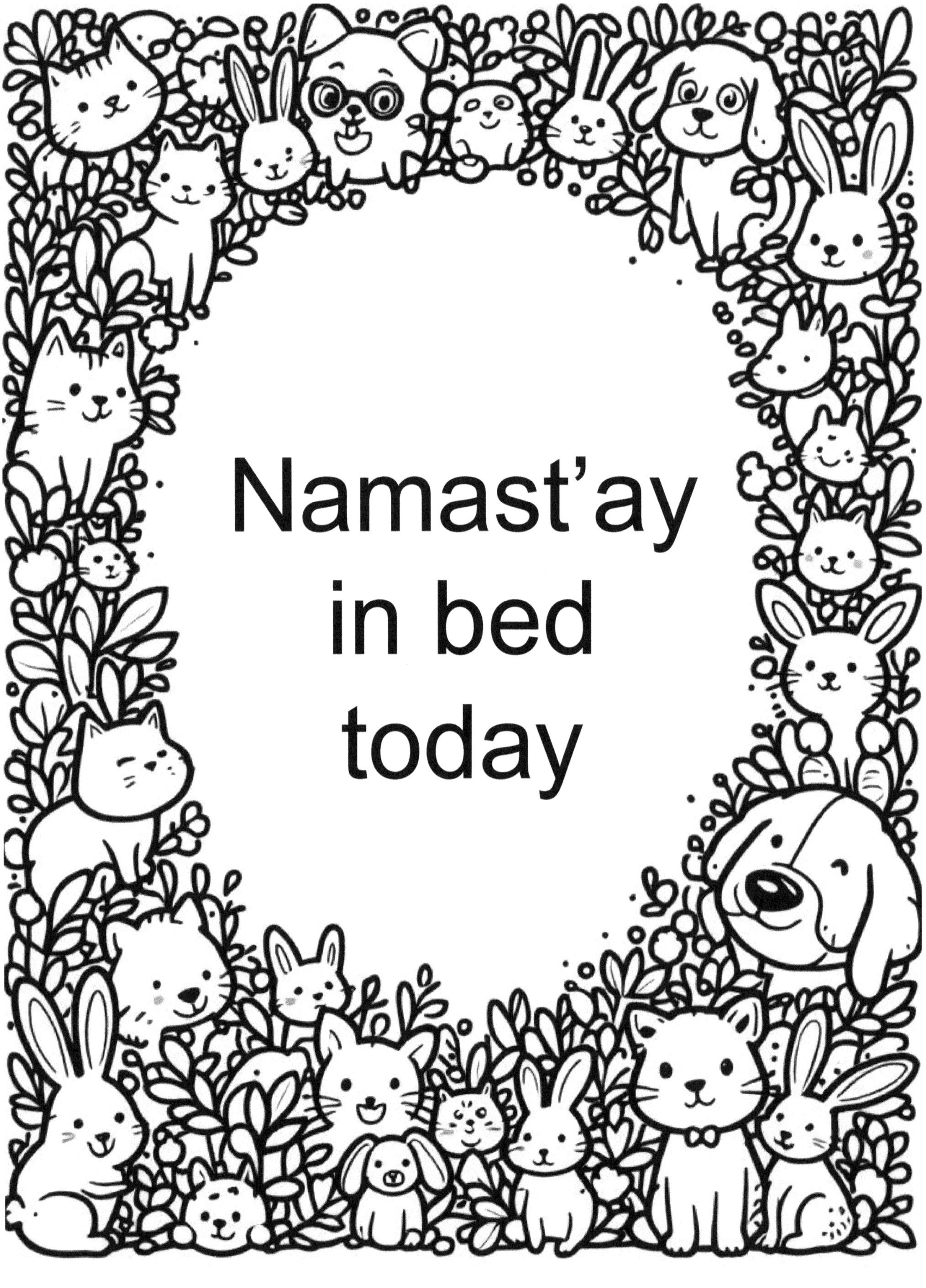

Namast’ay
in bed
today

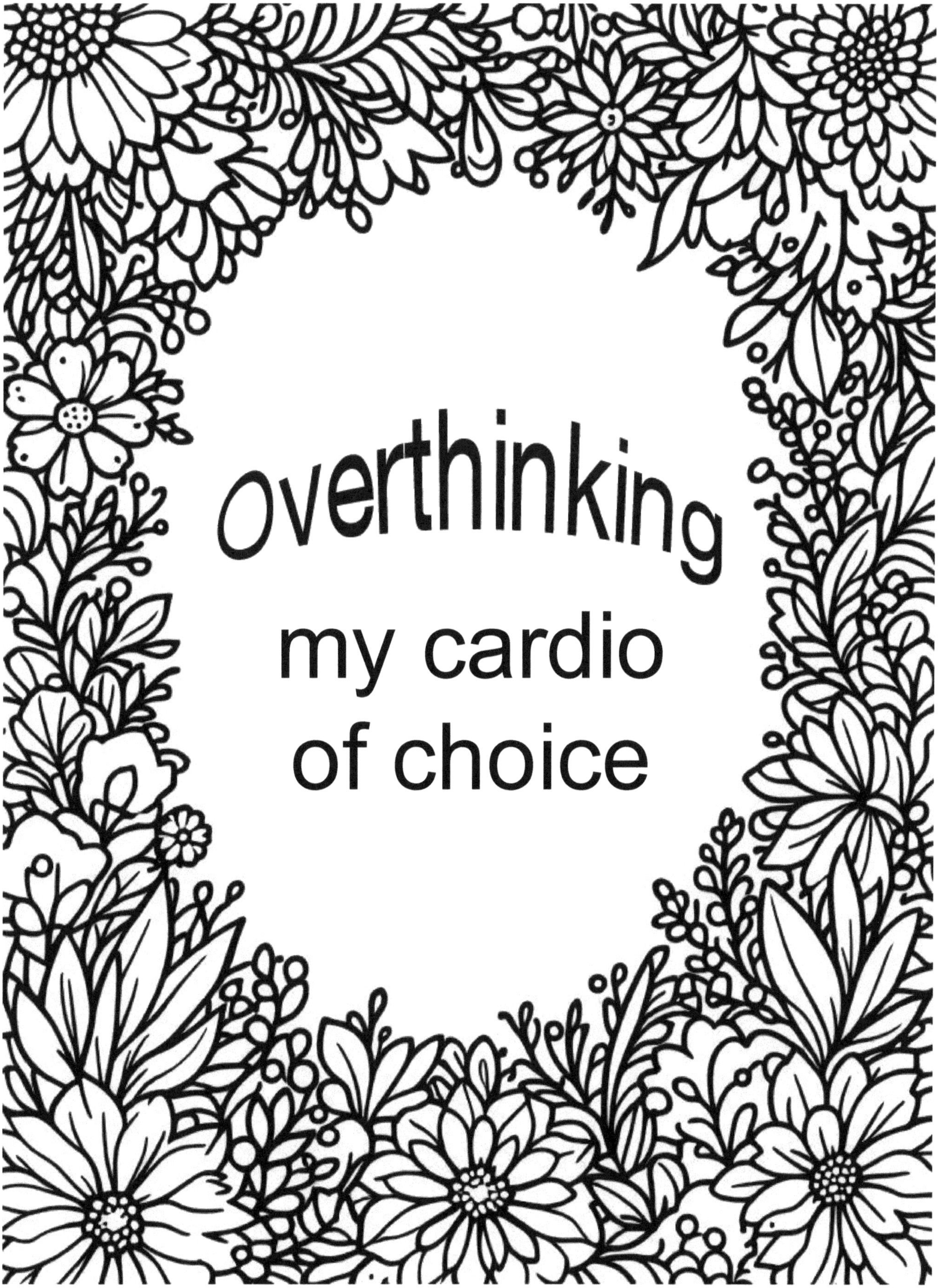
Overthinking
my cardio
of choice

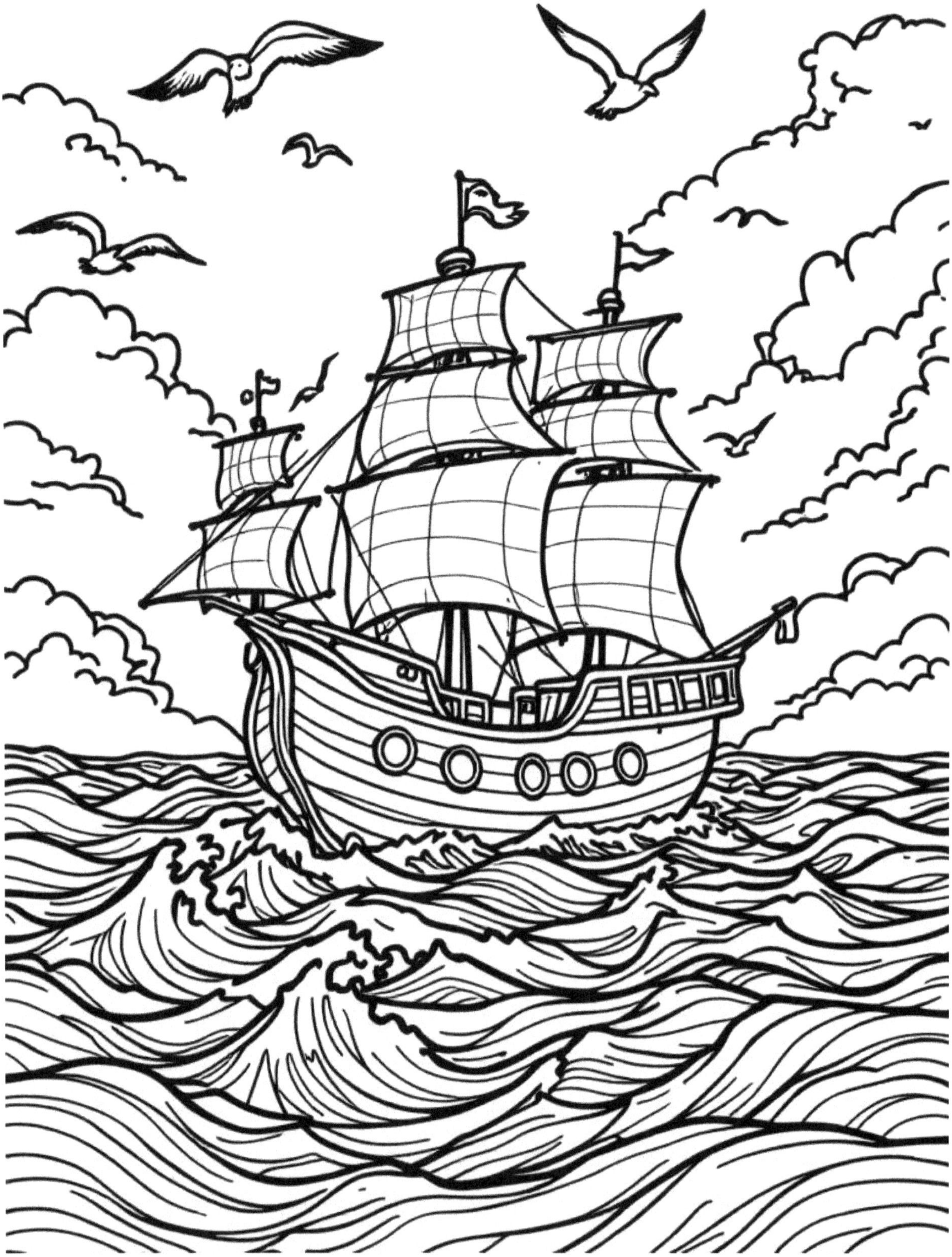

Namast'ay in Chaos: A Tale of Zen and Zany

Meet Lily, a millennial who describes herself as "thriving in chaos" but is really just over-caffeinated and slightly underachieving. Her life motto is, "Everything happens for a reason, and that reason is poor decisions."

The story begins on a Monday morning—because, of course, when else does disaster strike? Lily's week starts with an inspirational post-it note on her fridge: "Keep calm and wine on." It's not motivational per se, but it's her vibe. With her cat staring judgmentally from the counter, Lily mumbles her daily sarcastic affirmation: *"I'm thriving... probably. Maybe. Let's see."*

Just as she takes her first sip of coffee, her phone buzzes with a text from her boss: *"Need that report by 9 a.m."* She glances at the clock. It's 8:47. The report? It's still a vague idea floating somewhere between her last meltdown and her Netflix binge.

"No problem," Lily mutters, channeling the serenity of a stressed-out yoga instructor. She frantically types something that vaguely resembles coherent work and hits send. Crisis averted —until her cat knocks her coffee onto the keyboard. "You little chaos gremlin!" she shouts as the laptop sparks dramatically.

Continue on p28

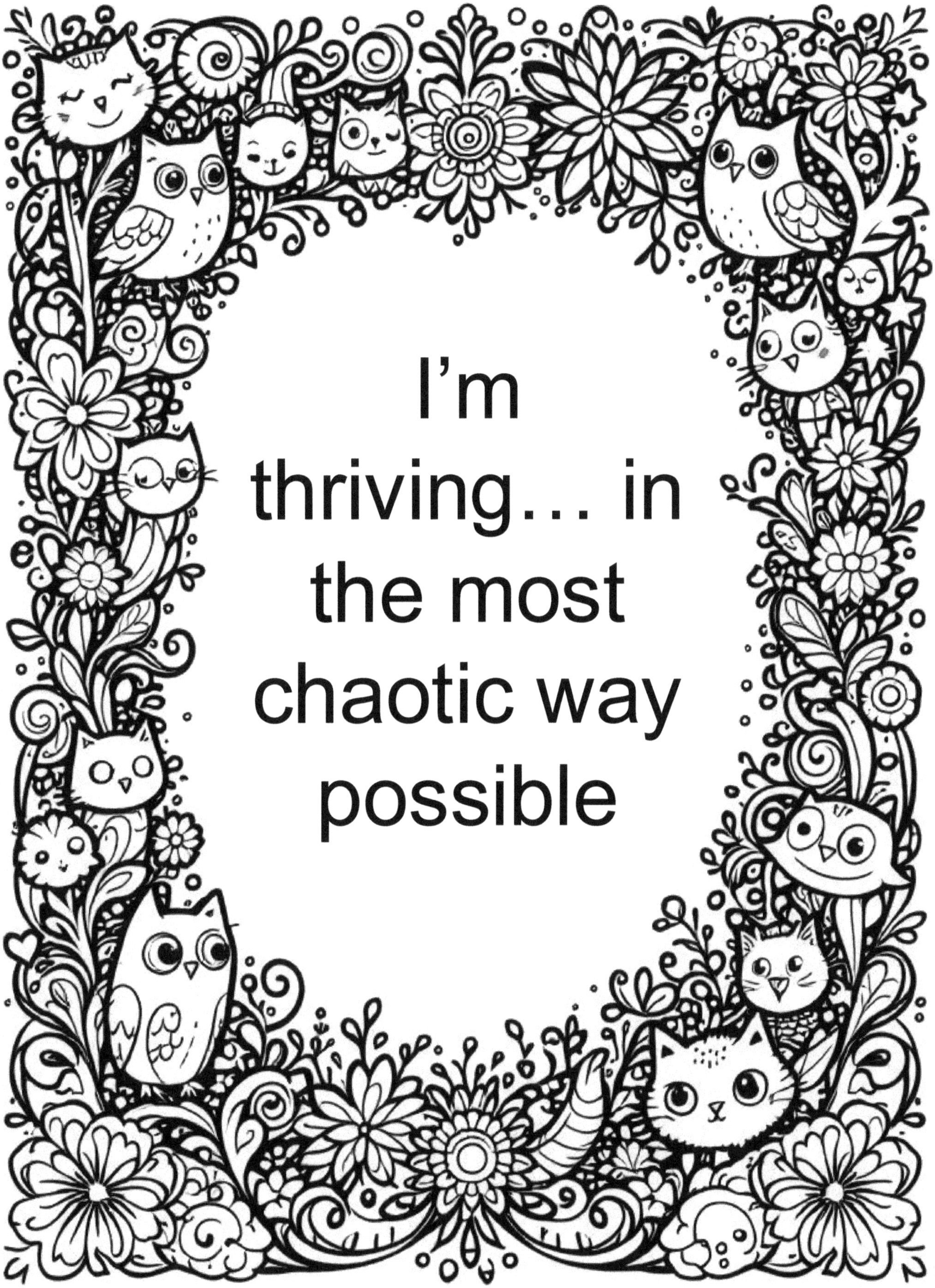

I'm thriving… in the most chaotic way possible

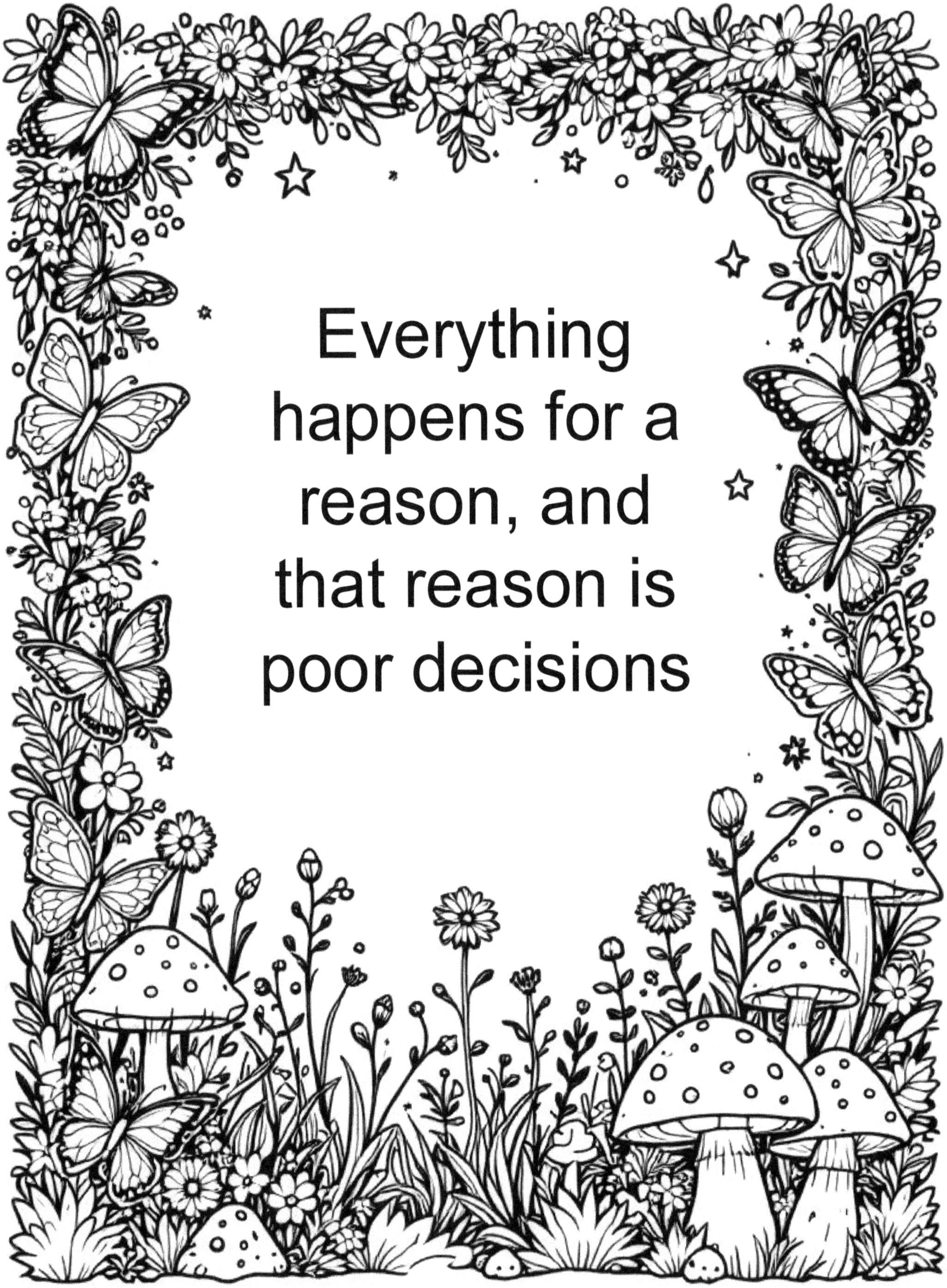

Everything happens for a reason, and that reason is poor decisions

Stress spelled backward is desserts. Coincidence ?

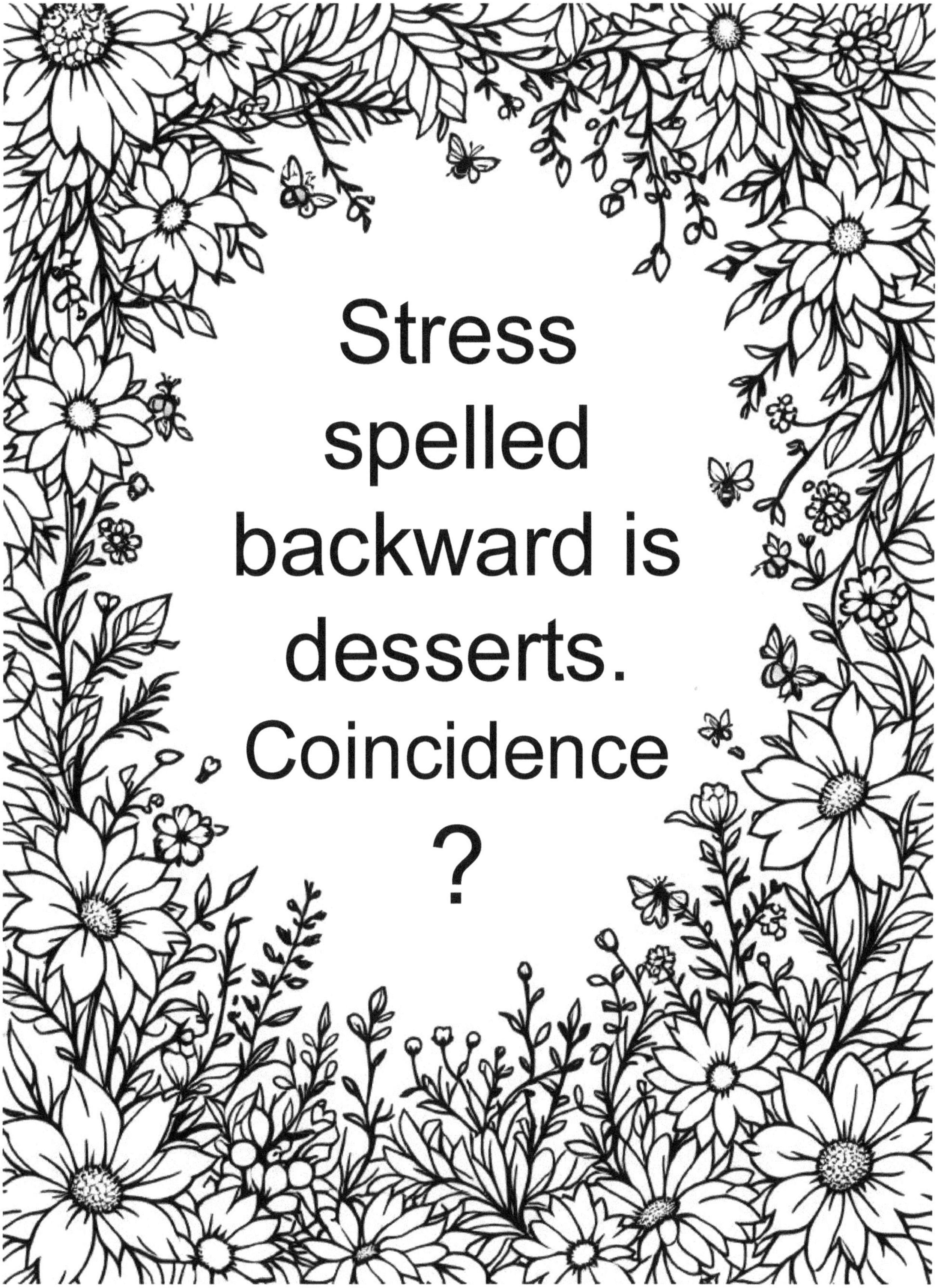

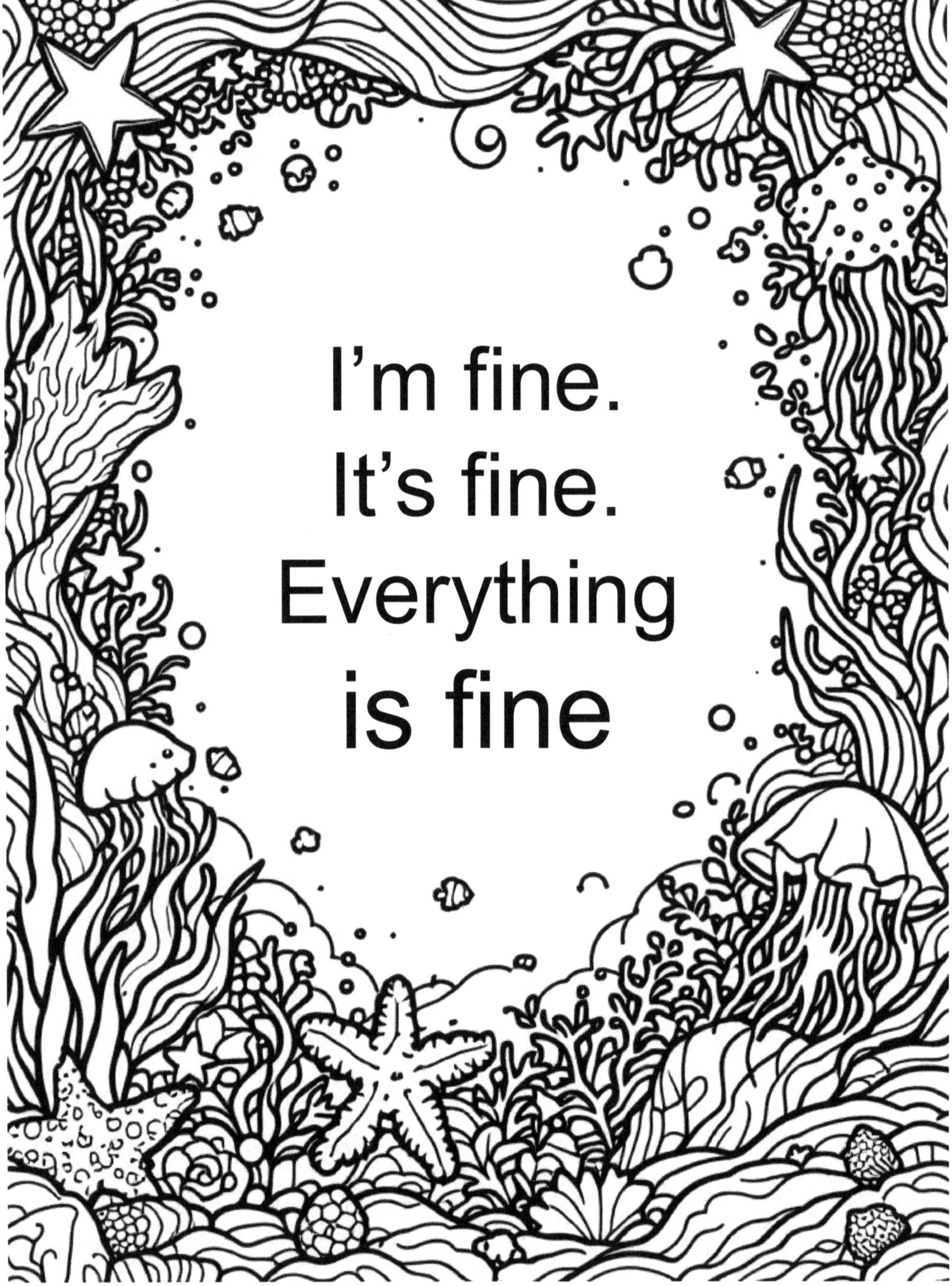
I’m fine.
It’s fine.
Everything
is fine

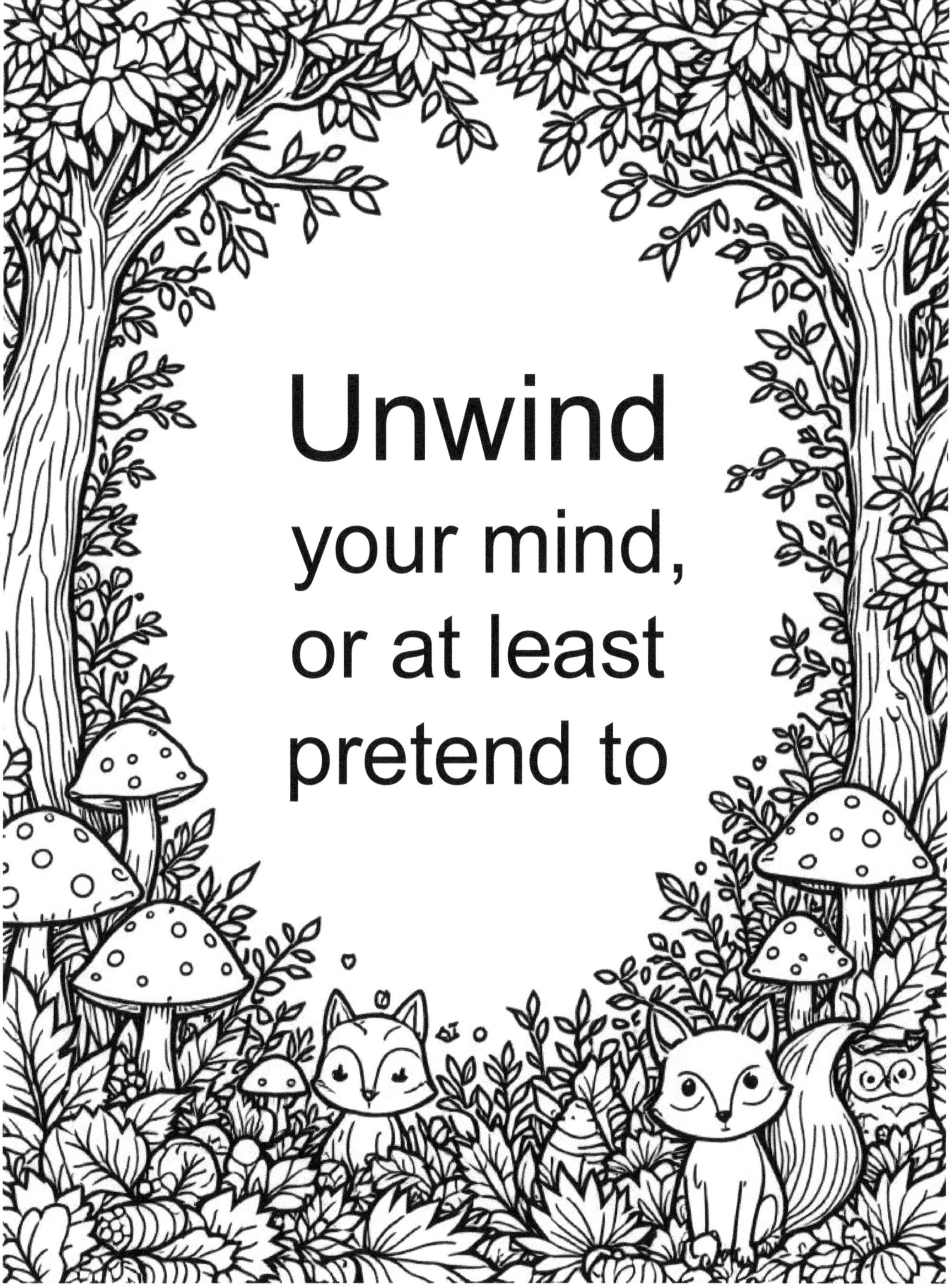

Unwind

your mind,
or at least
pretend to

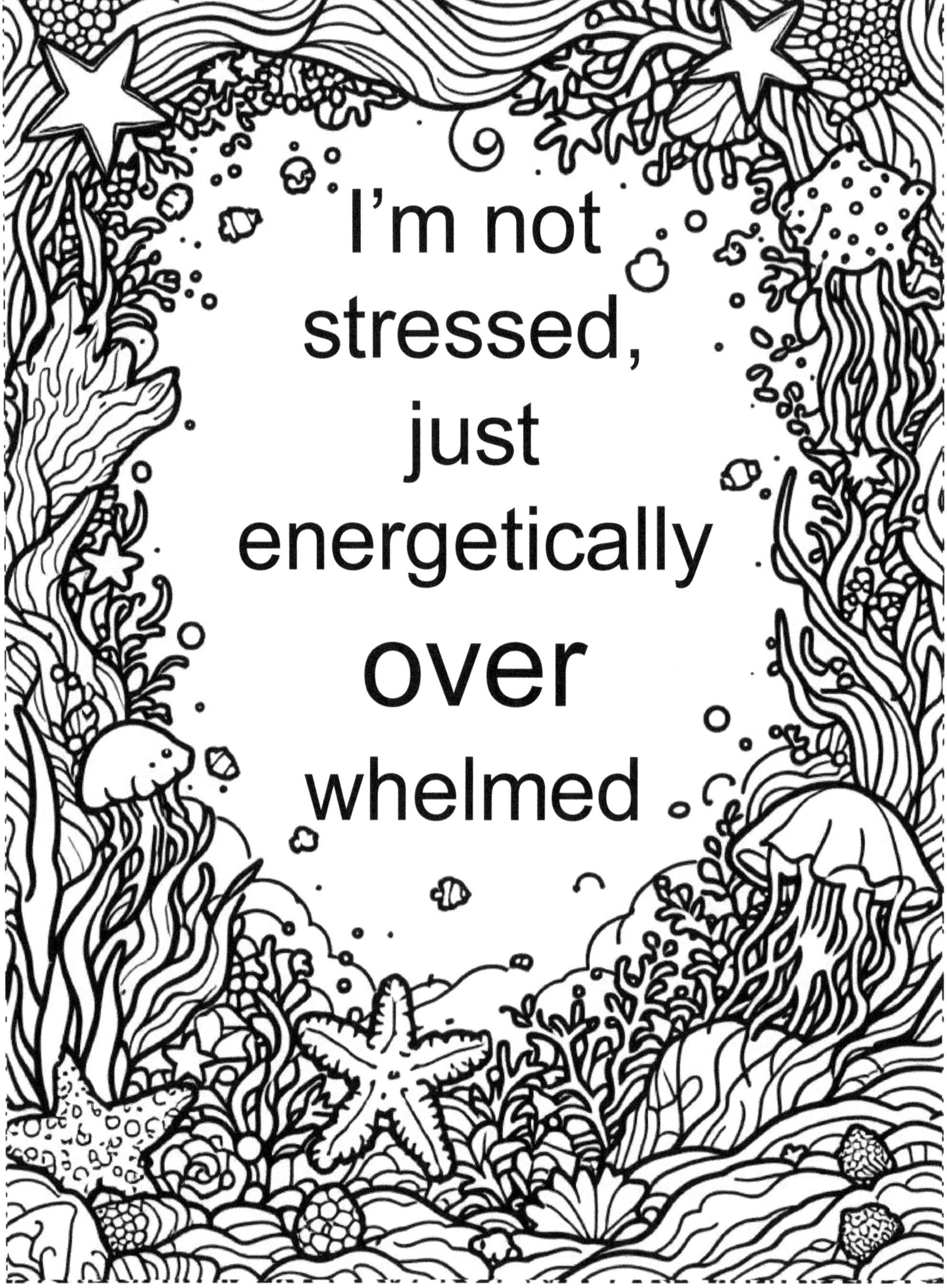
I'm not
stressed,
just
energetically
over
whelmed

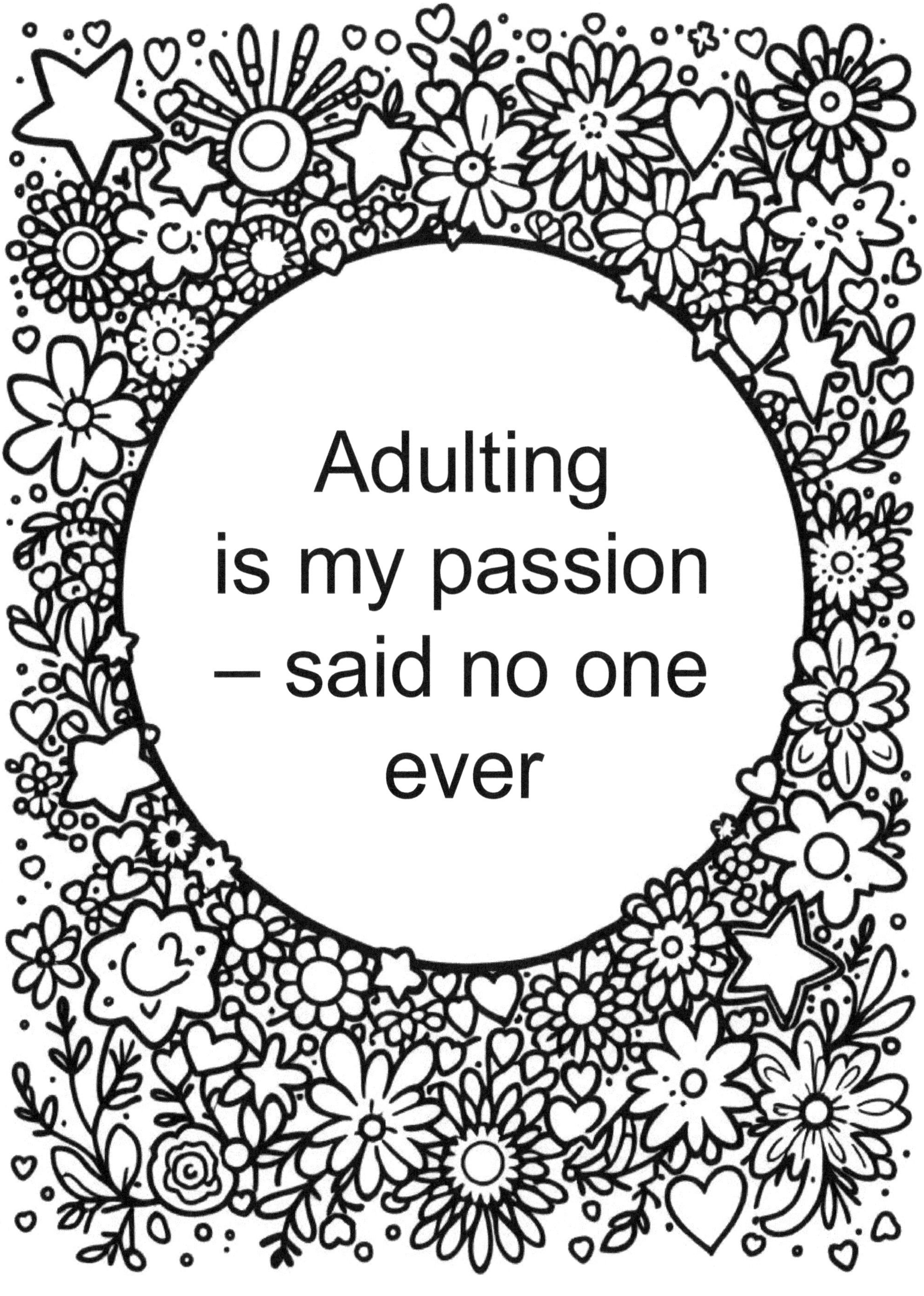
Adulting
is my passion
– said no one
ever

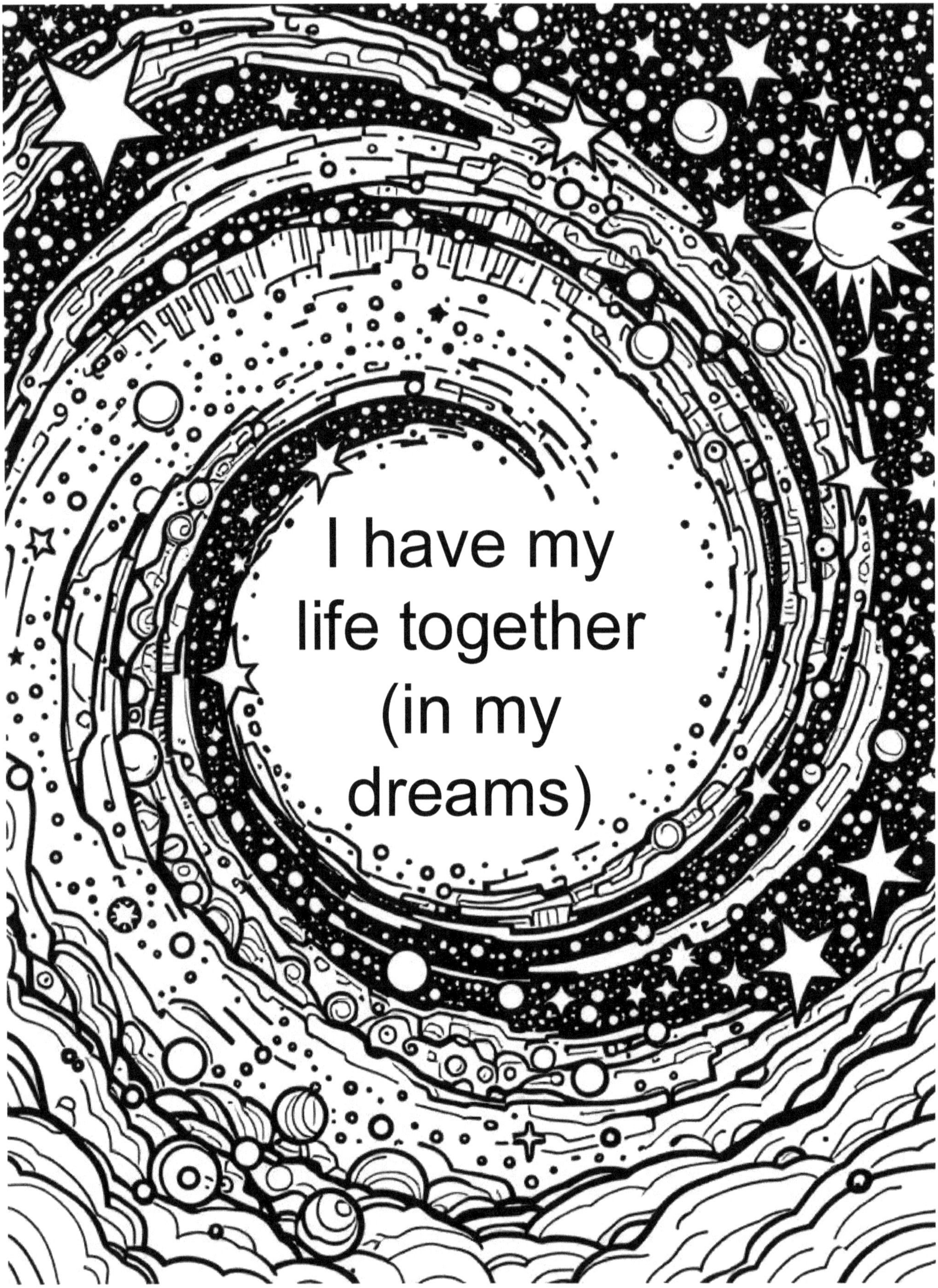
I have my
life together
(in my
dreams)

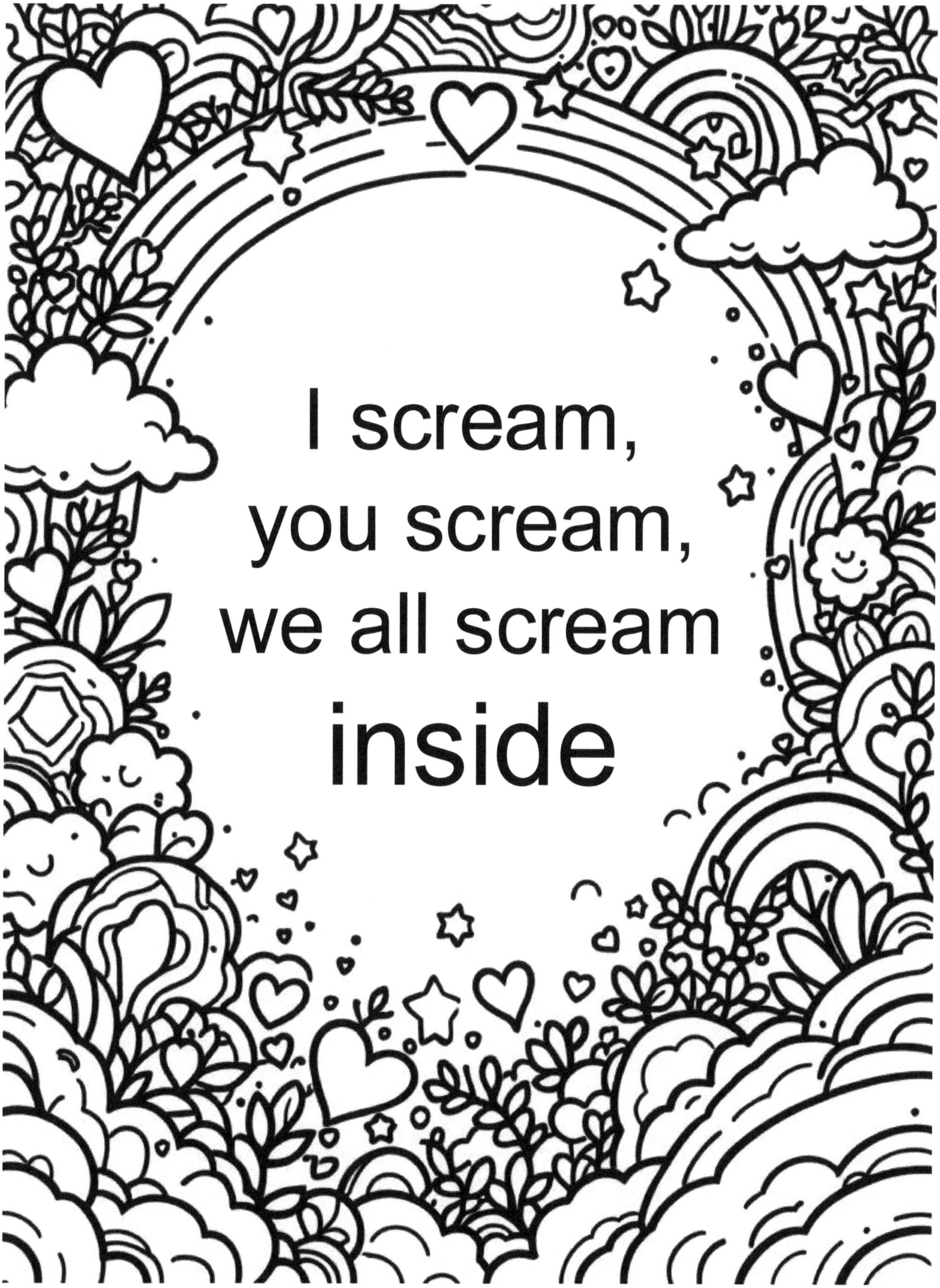
I scream,
you scream,
we all scream
inside

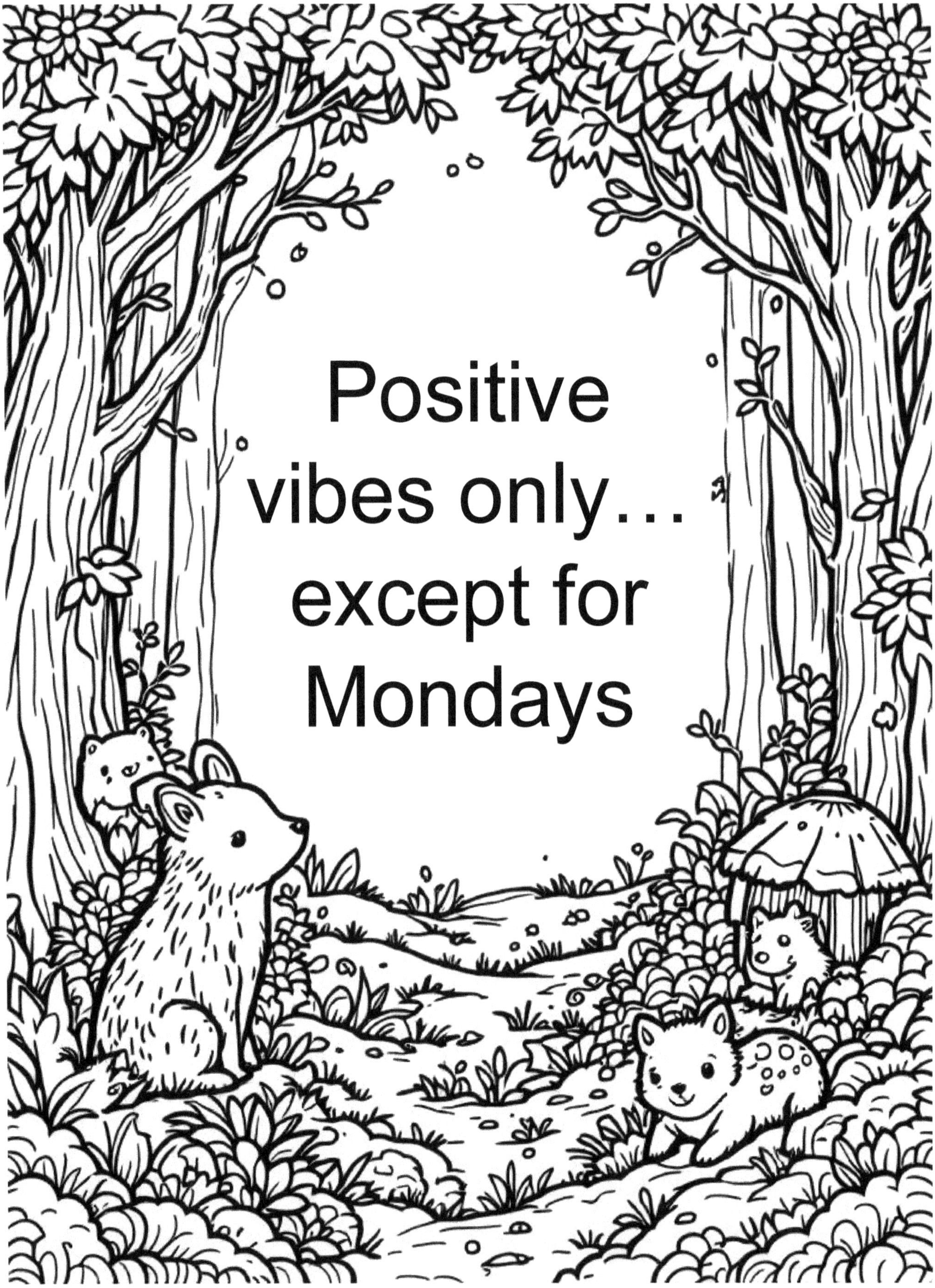
Positive
vibes only…
except for
Mondays

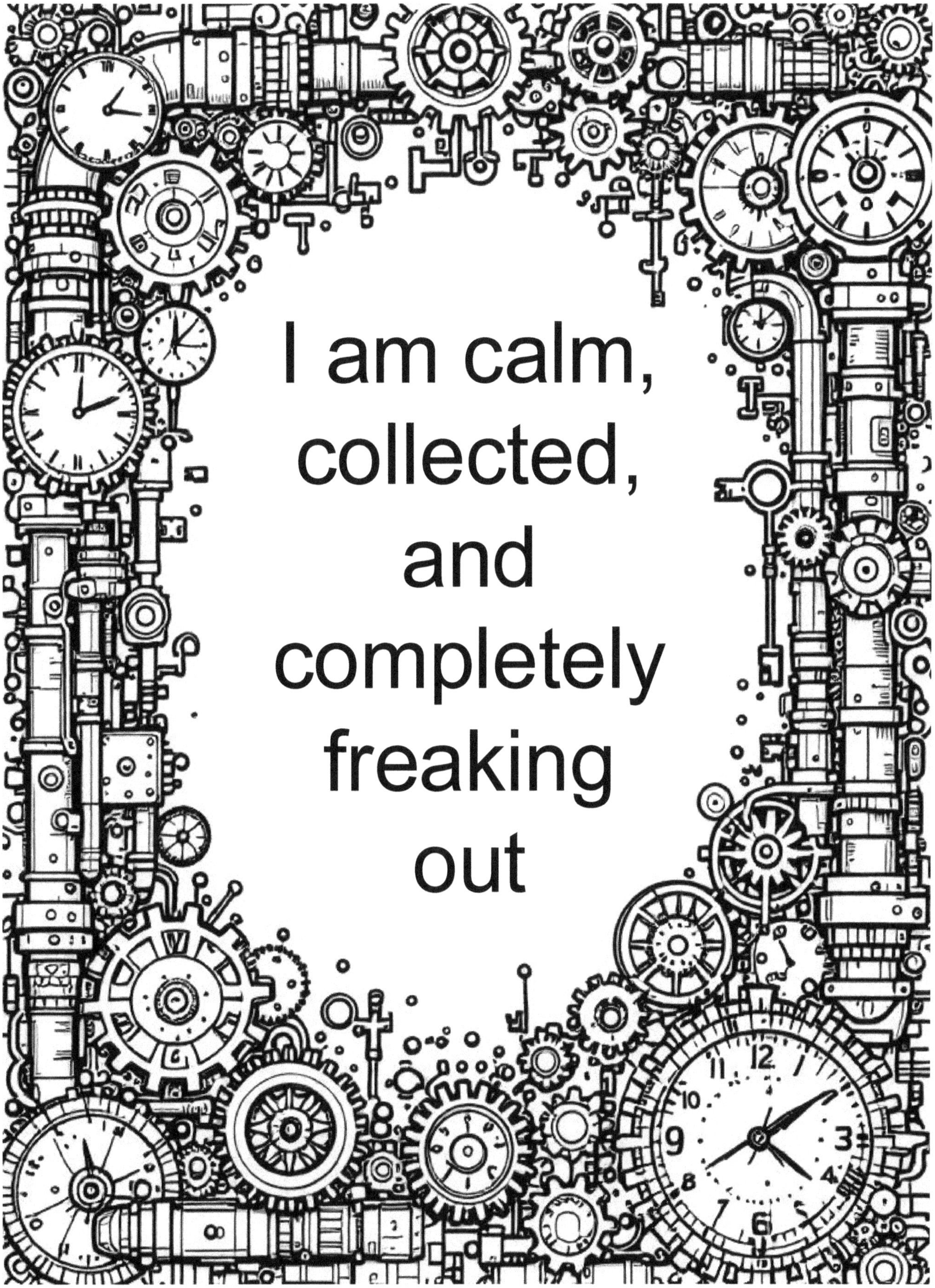

I am calm,
collected,
and
completely
freaking
out

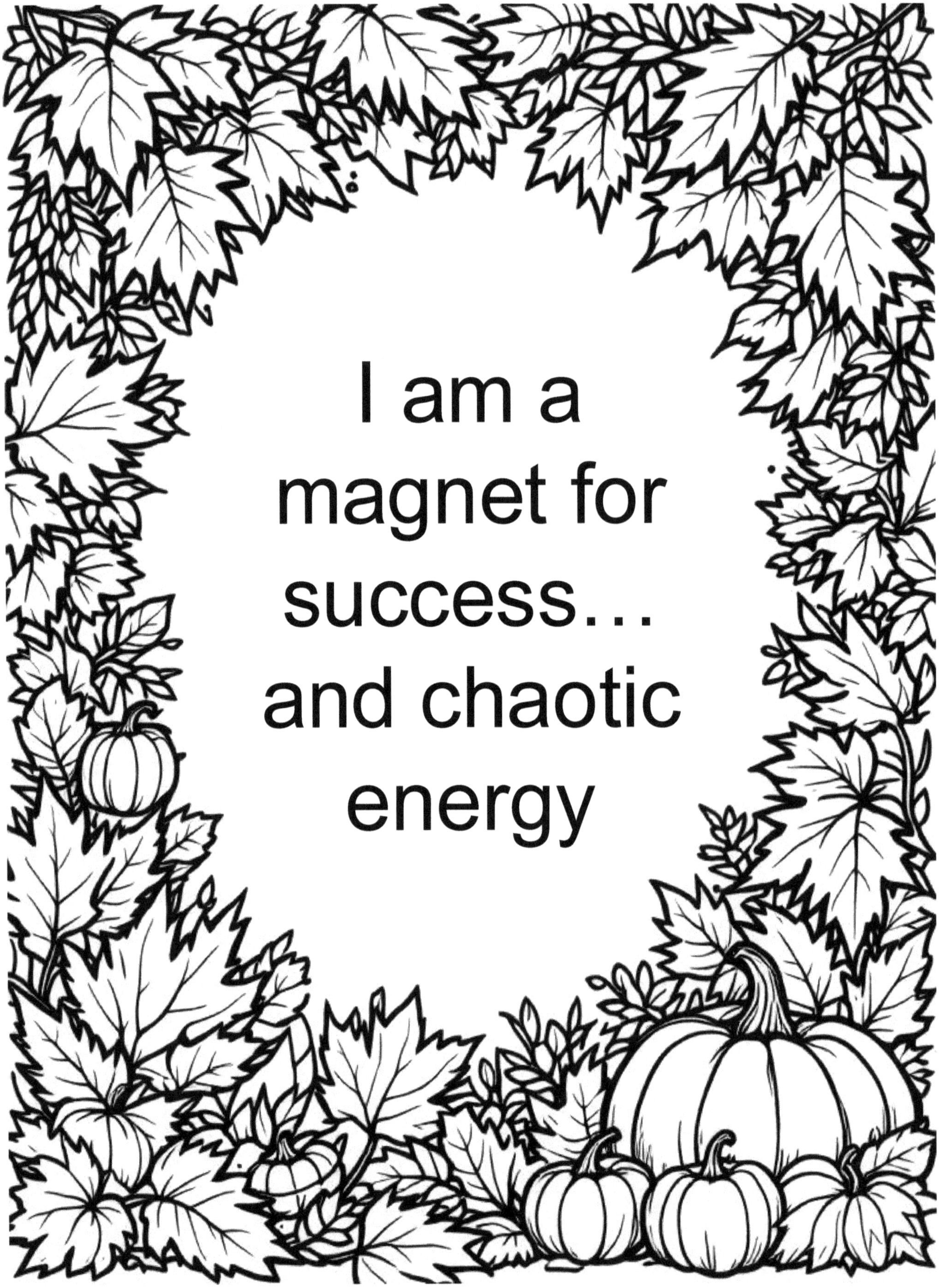
I am a
magnet for
success…
and chaotic
energy

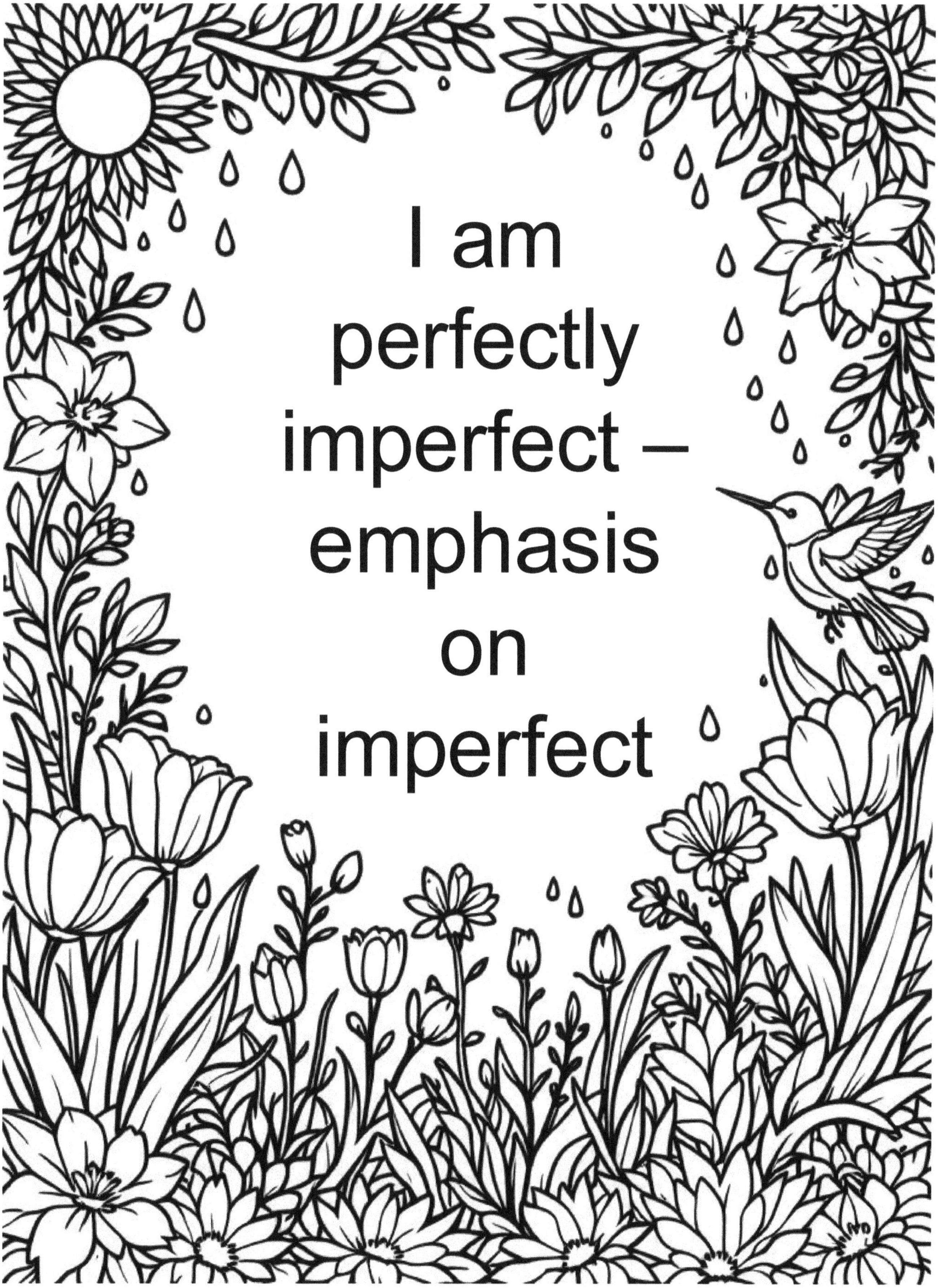
I am
perfectly
imperfect –
emphasis
on
imperfect

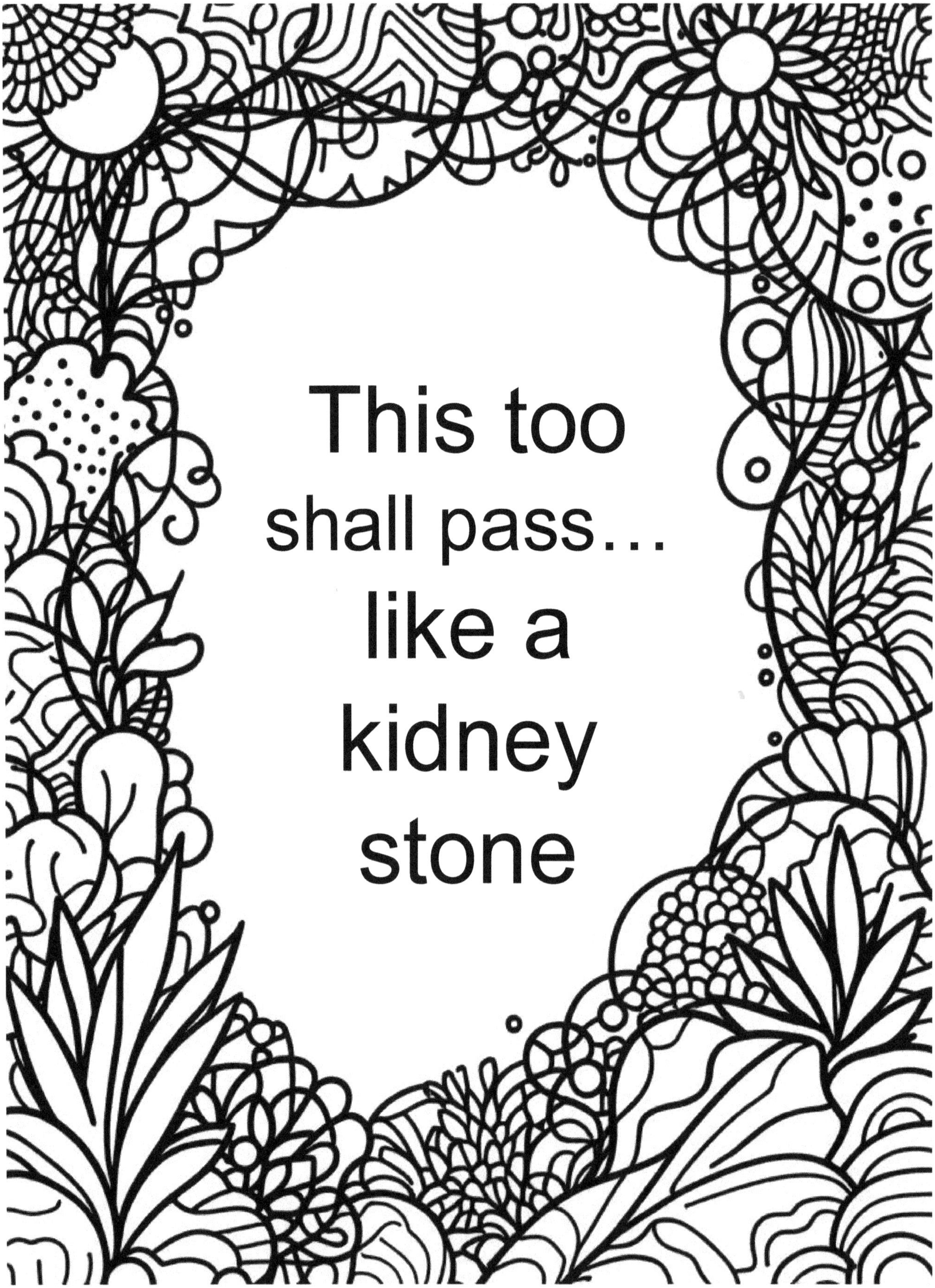
This too
shall pass…
like a
kidney
stone

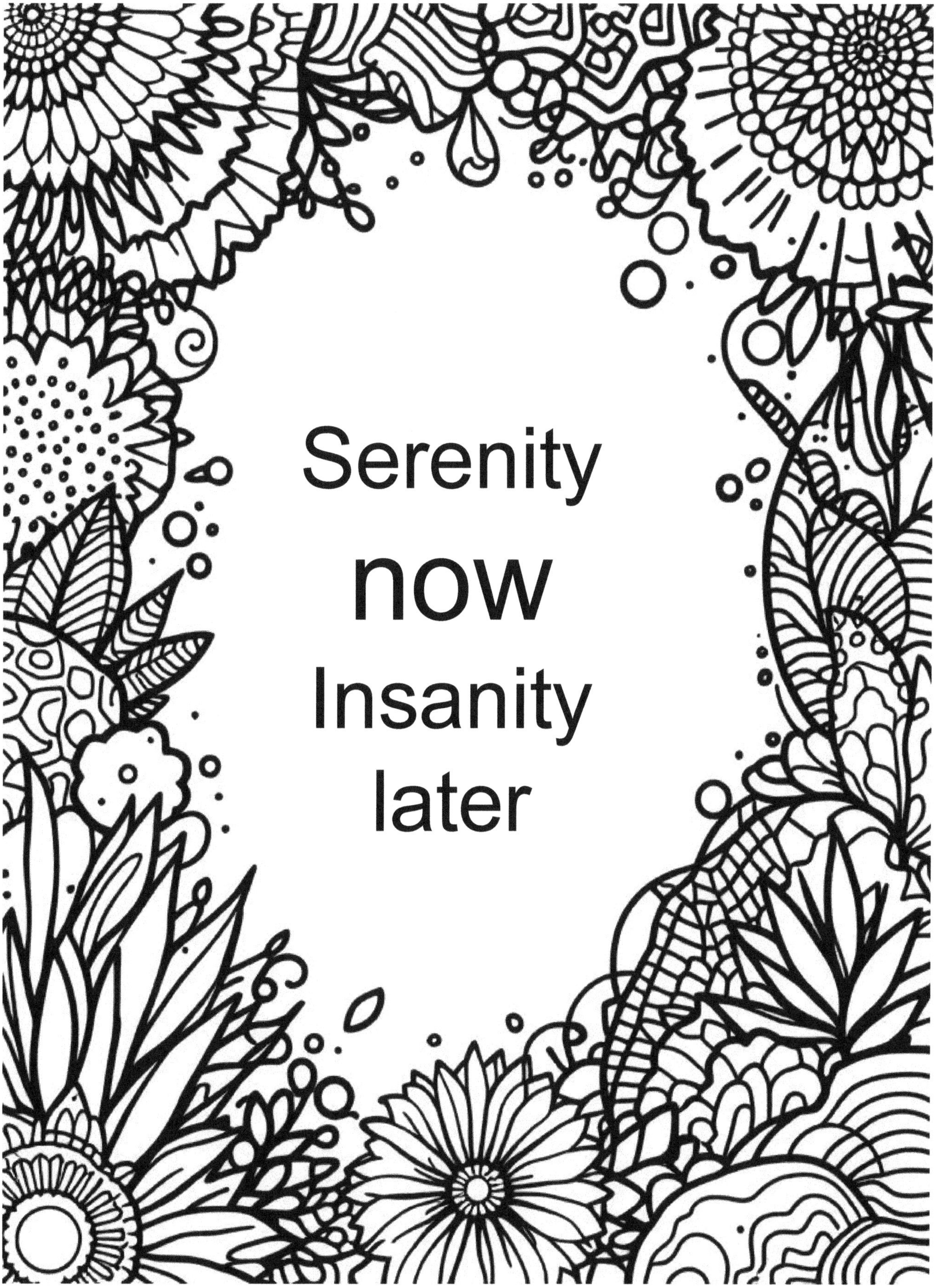
Serenity
now
Insanity
later

That evening, after a day of *thriving in organized stress,* Lily decides to unwind. She lights a candle, puts on some calming music, and opens her adult coloring book, titled "*Serenity Now, Insanity Later.*" She's coloring in a sarcastic affirmation that reads: *"This too shall pass... like a kidney stone,"* when her phone dings with a notification from her fitness app: *"You've walked 327 steps today. Keep moving!"*

"That's it," Lily sighs. "I'm officially a potato."

Deciding to "manifest a healthier lifestyle," she dusts off her yoga mat and searches for a beginner video. The instructor, a perky influencer named Celeste, greets her with a glowing smile: "Namaste! Find your center and release all your tension."

Lily tries, she really does, but five minutes in, she's tangled in downward dog, questioning life choices. Her cat climbs onto her back, mistaking her for a piece of furniture. "This is fine," Lily grumbles. "Totally zen."

Continue on p42

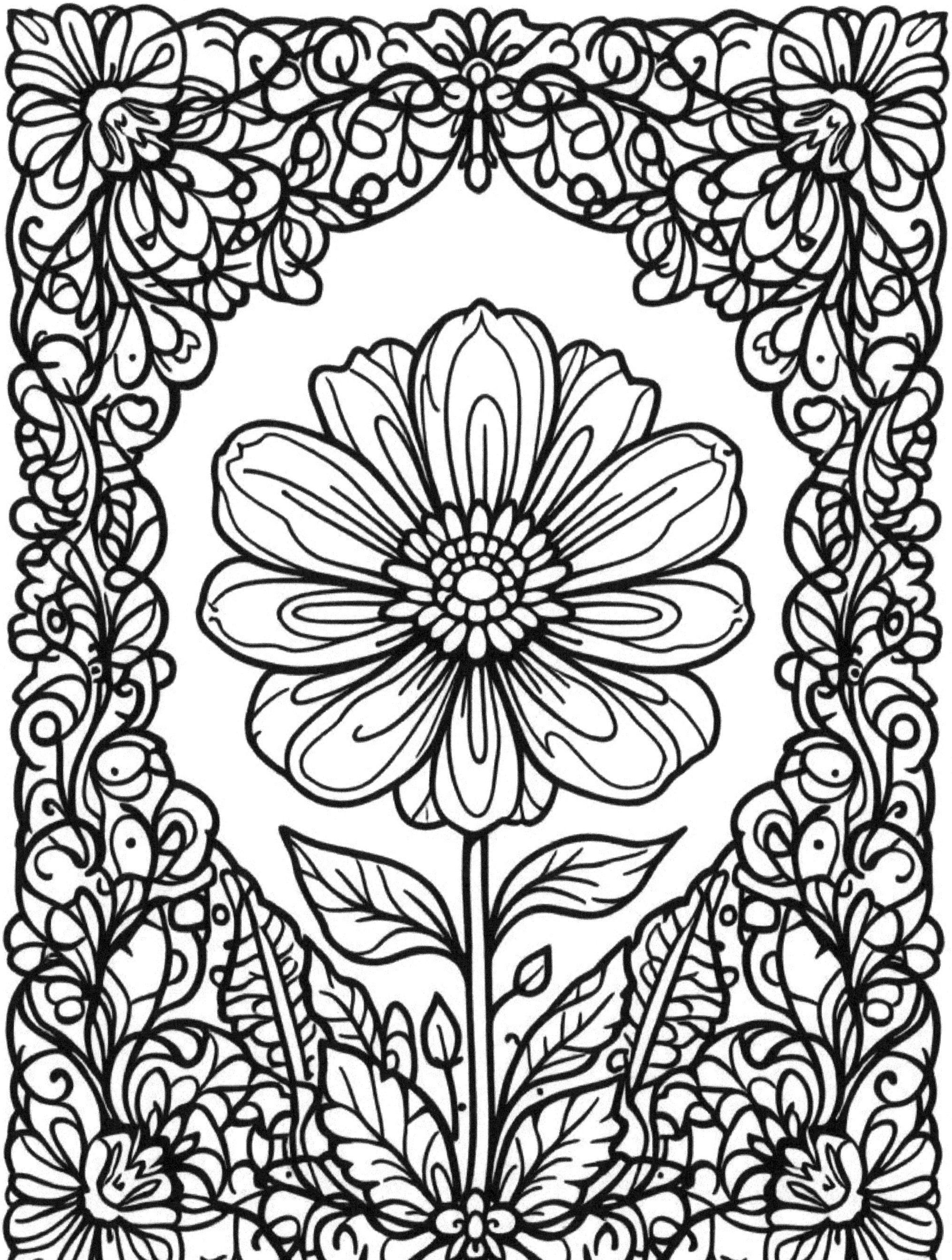

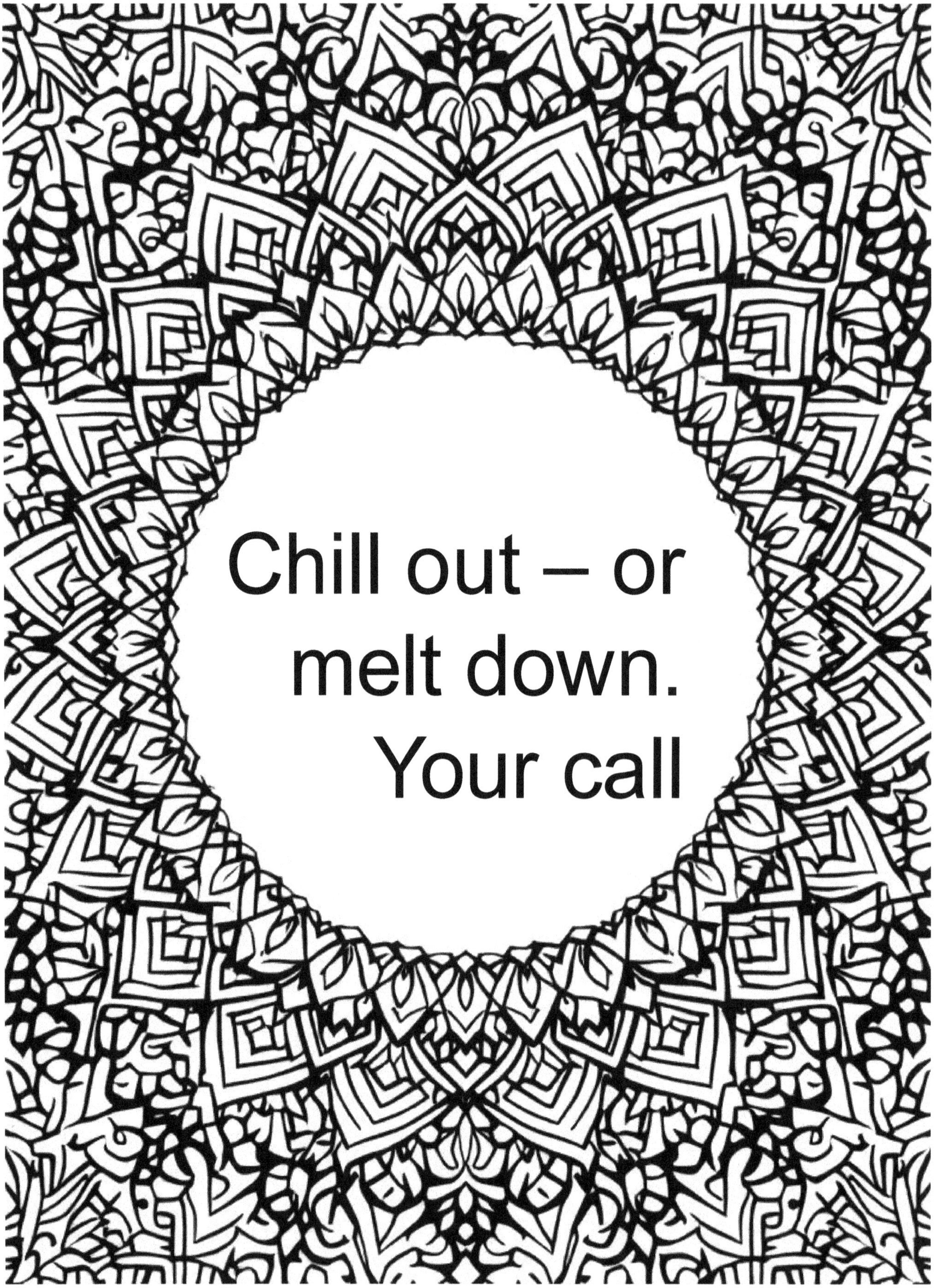
Chill out – or
melt down.
Your call

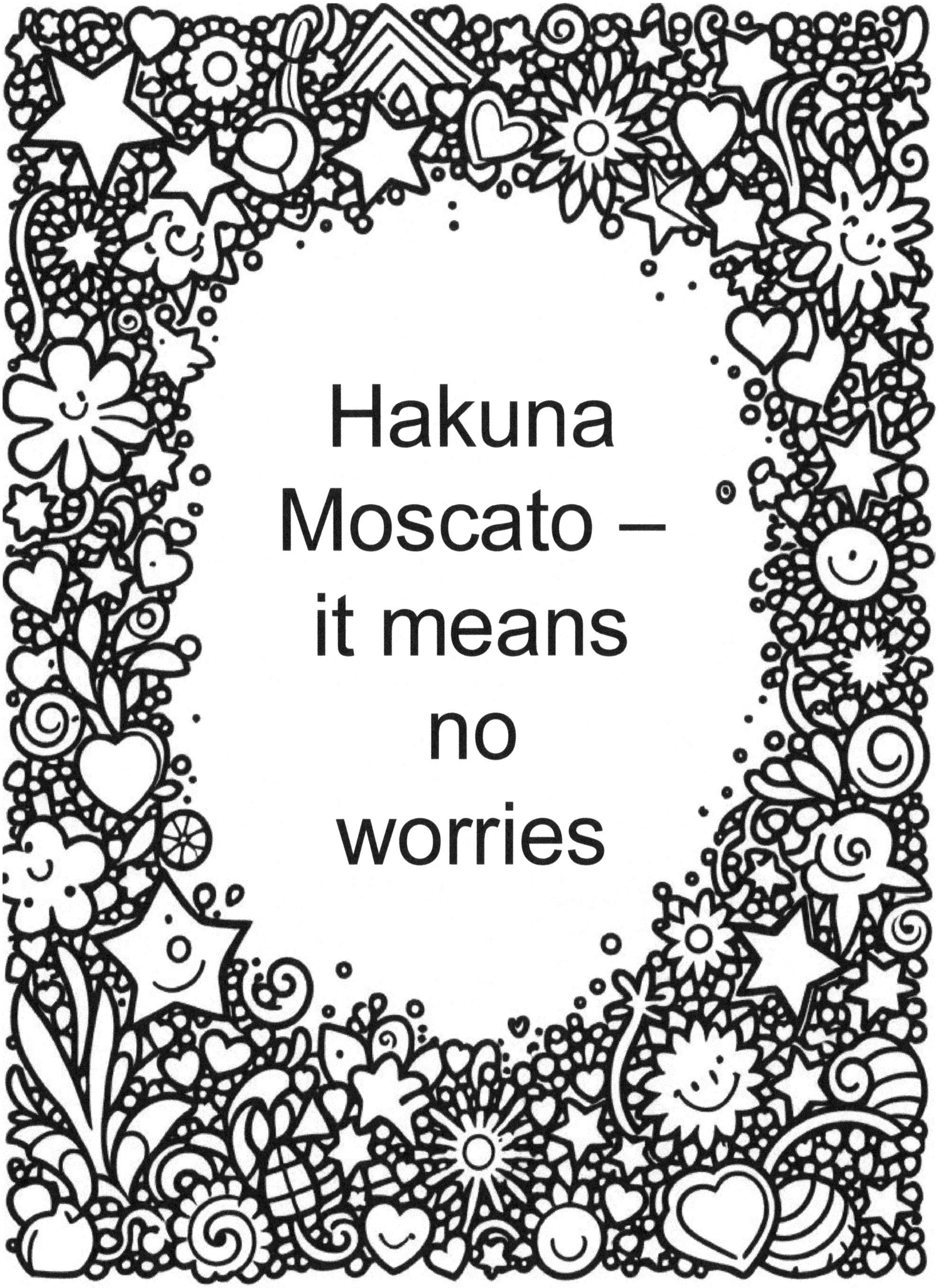

Hakuna Moscato – it means no worries

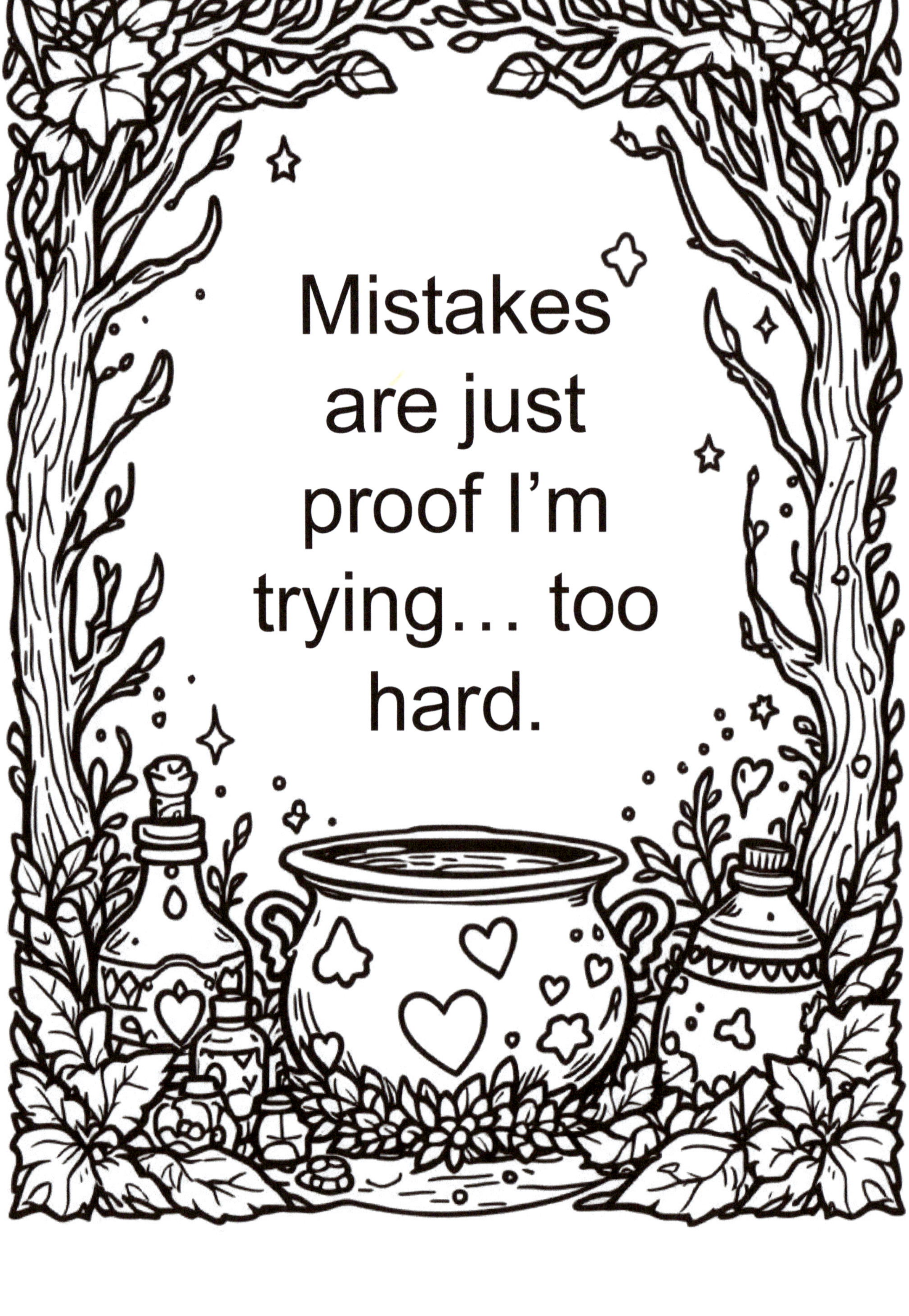
Mistakes are just proof I’m trying… too hard.

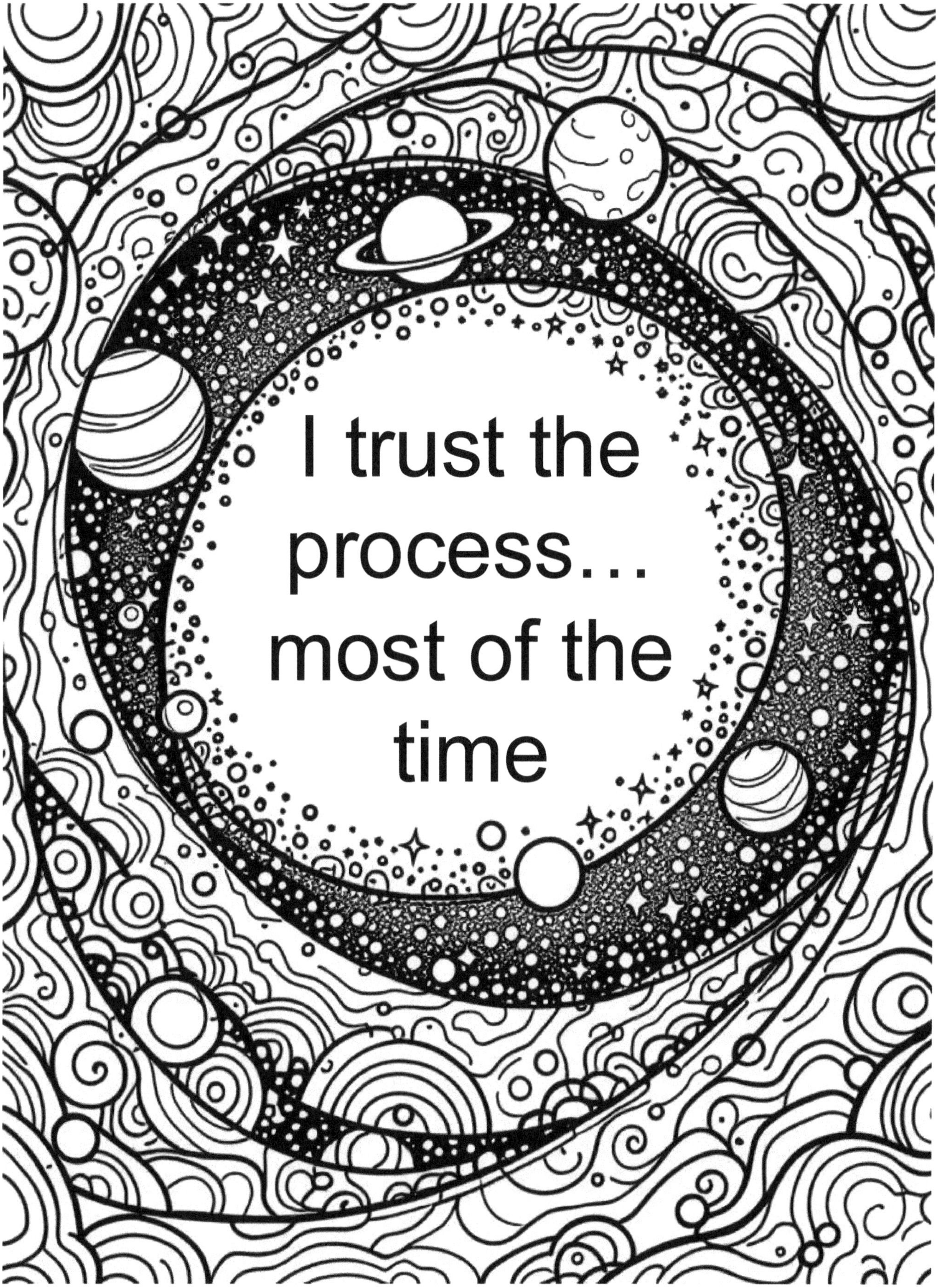
I trust the process… most of the time

Manifesting a nap and a million dollars

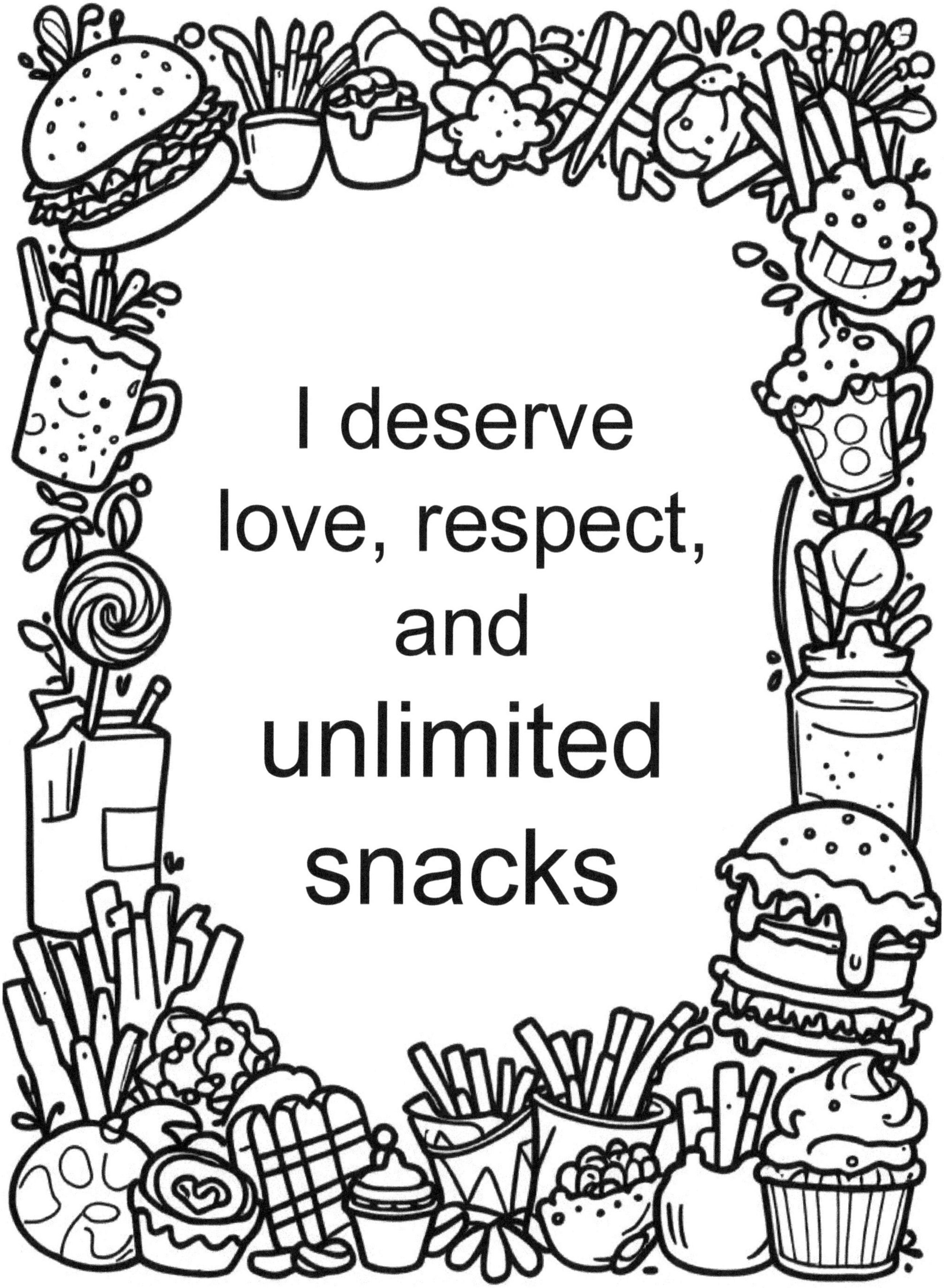
I deserve
love, respect,
and
unlimited
snacks

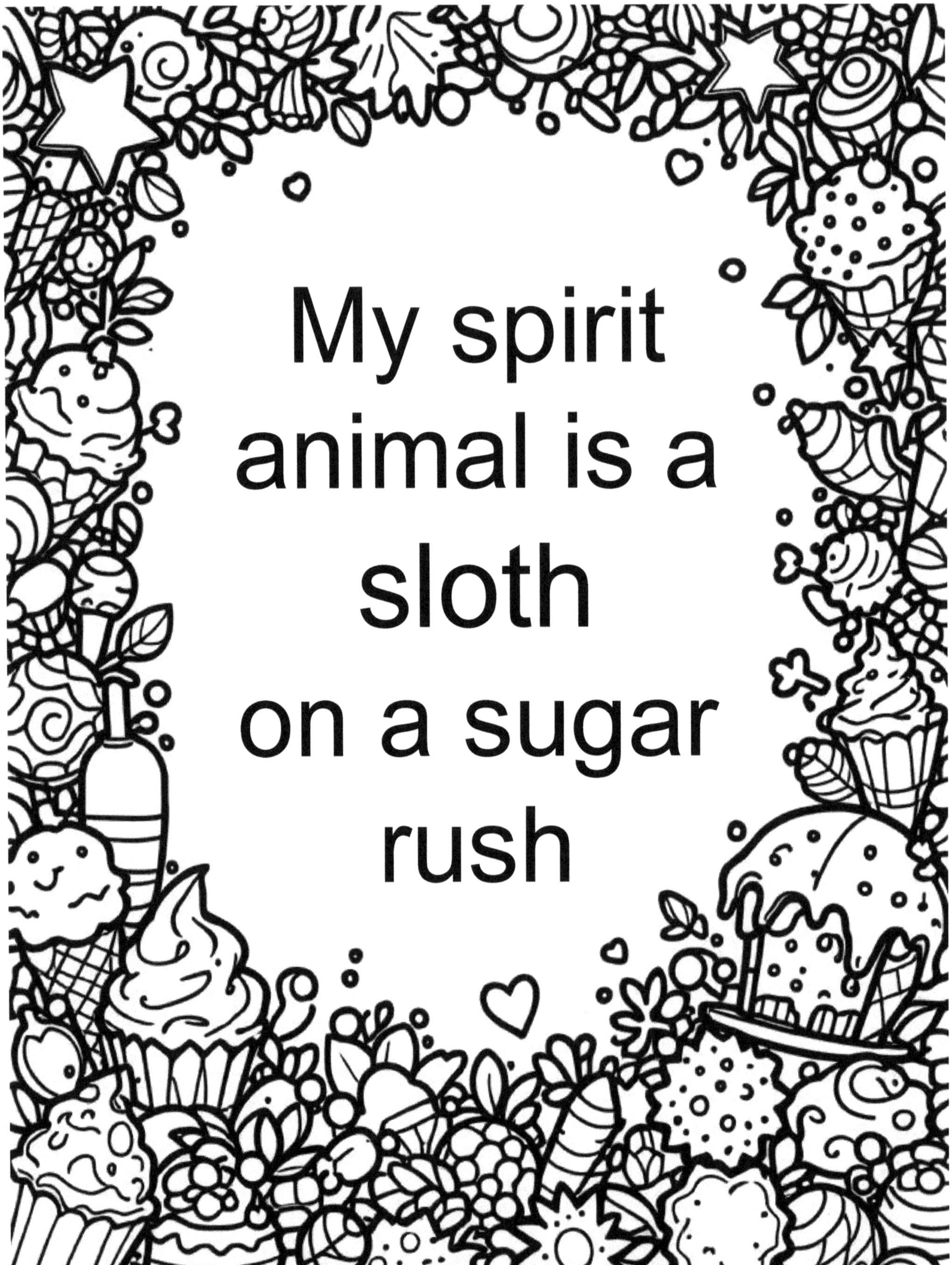

My spirit
animal is a
sloth
on a sugar
rush

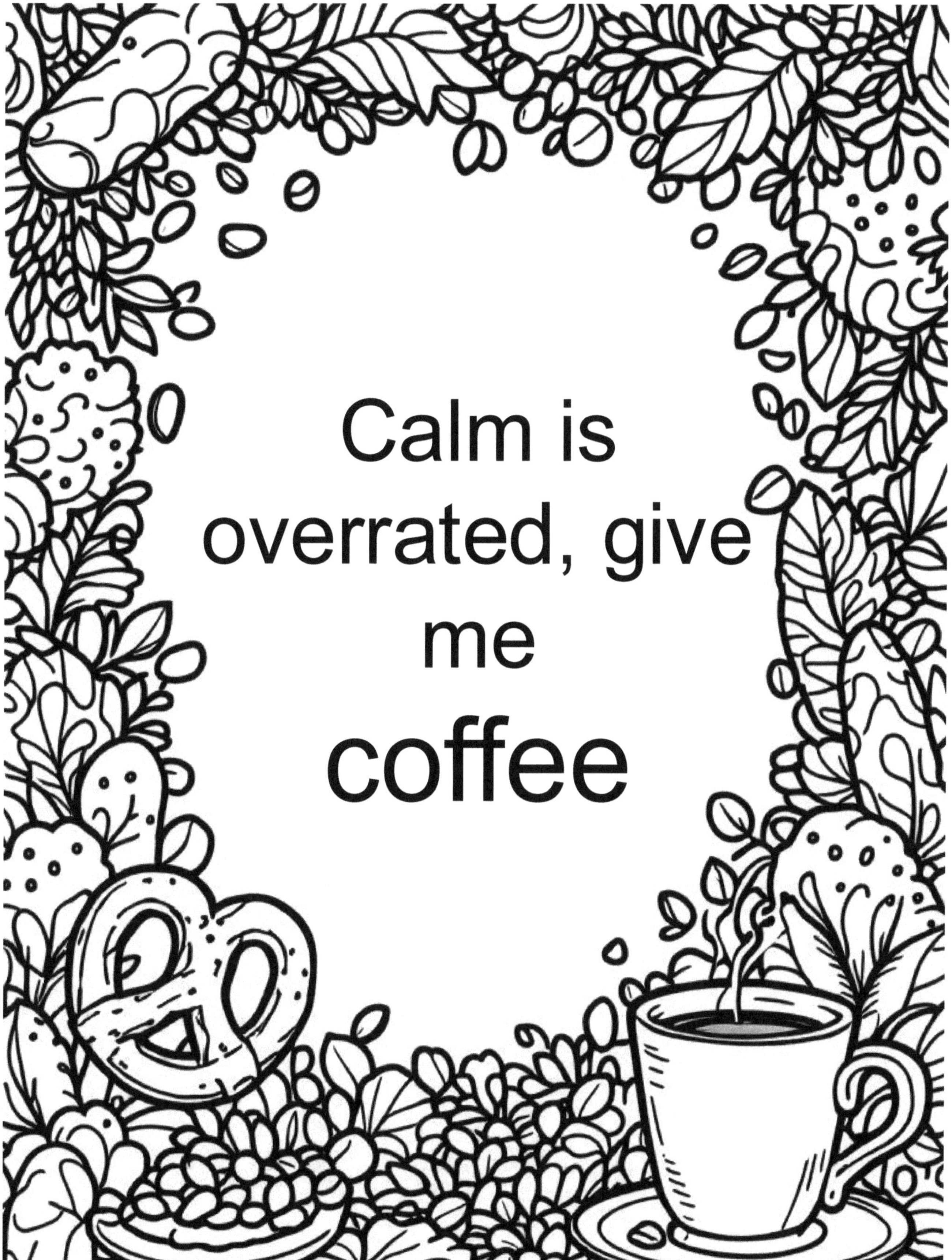
Calm is overrated, give me
coffee

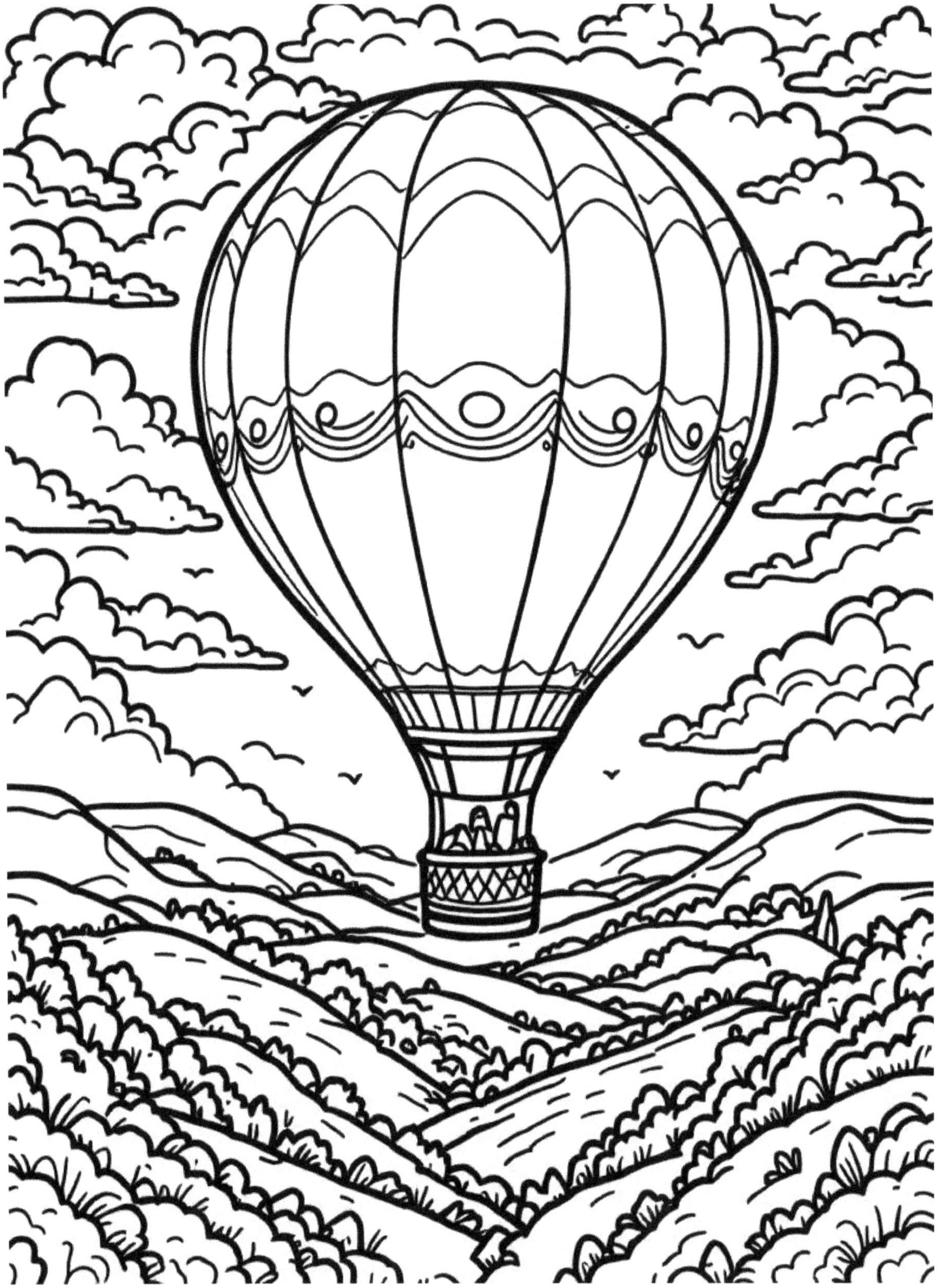

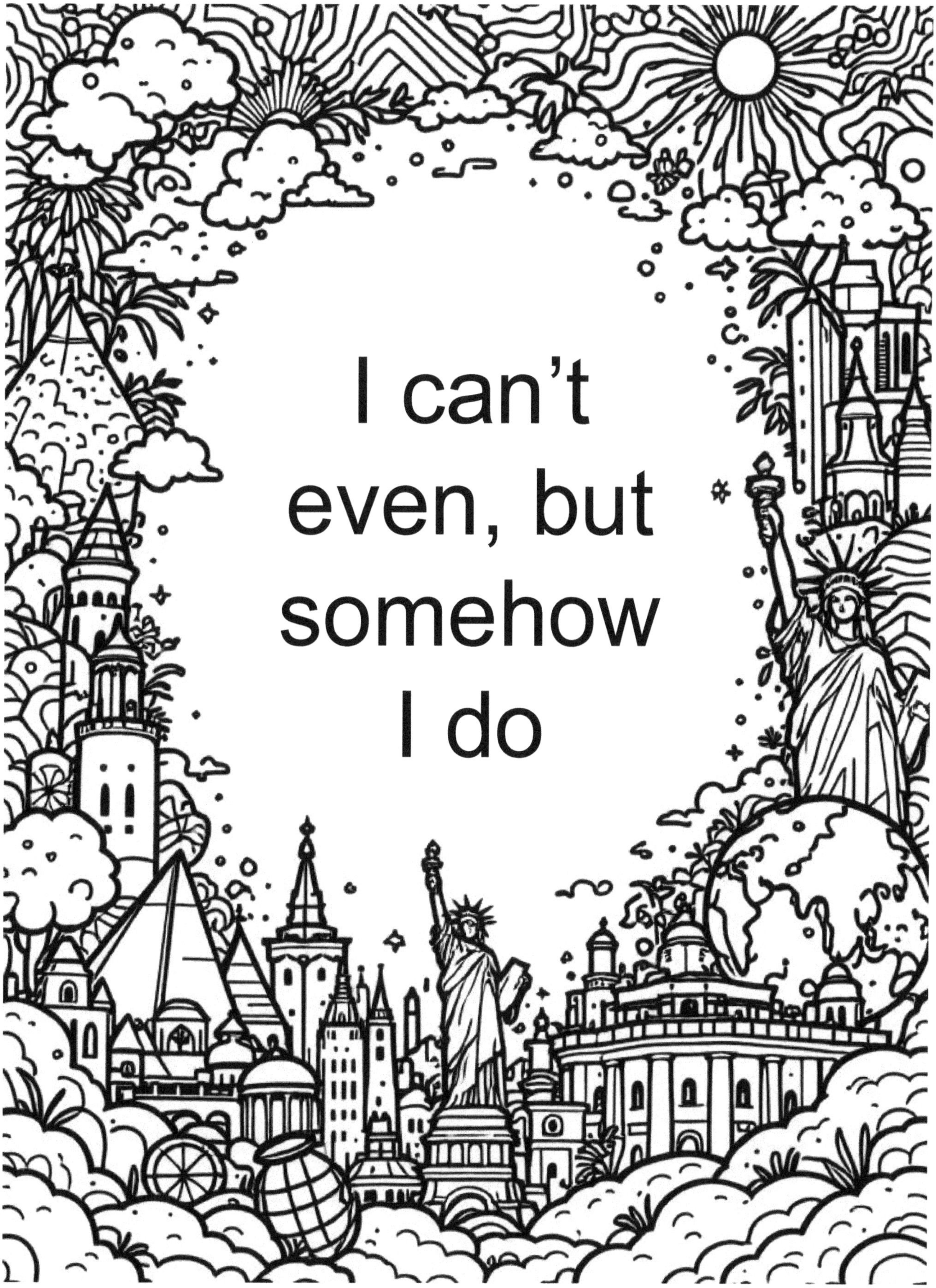
I can’t
even, but
somehow
I do

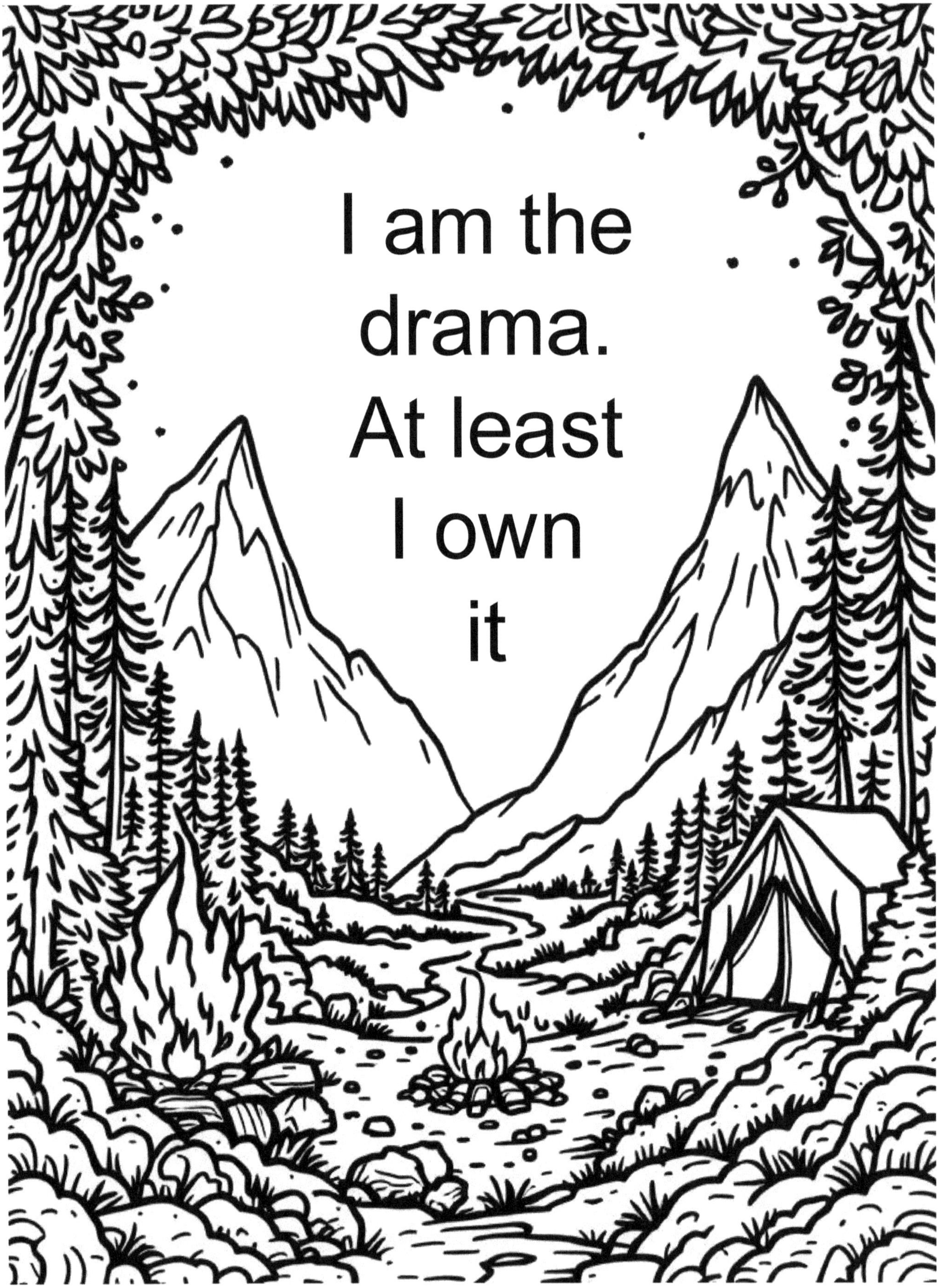
I am the
drama.
At least
I own
it

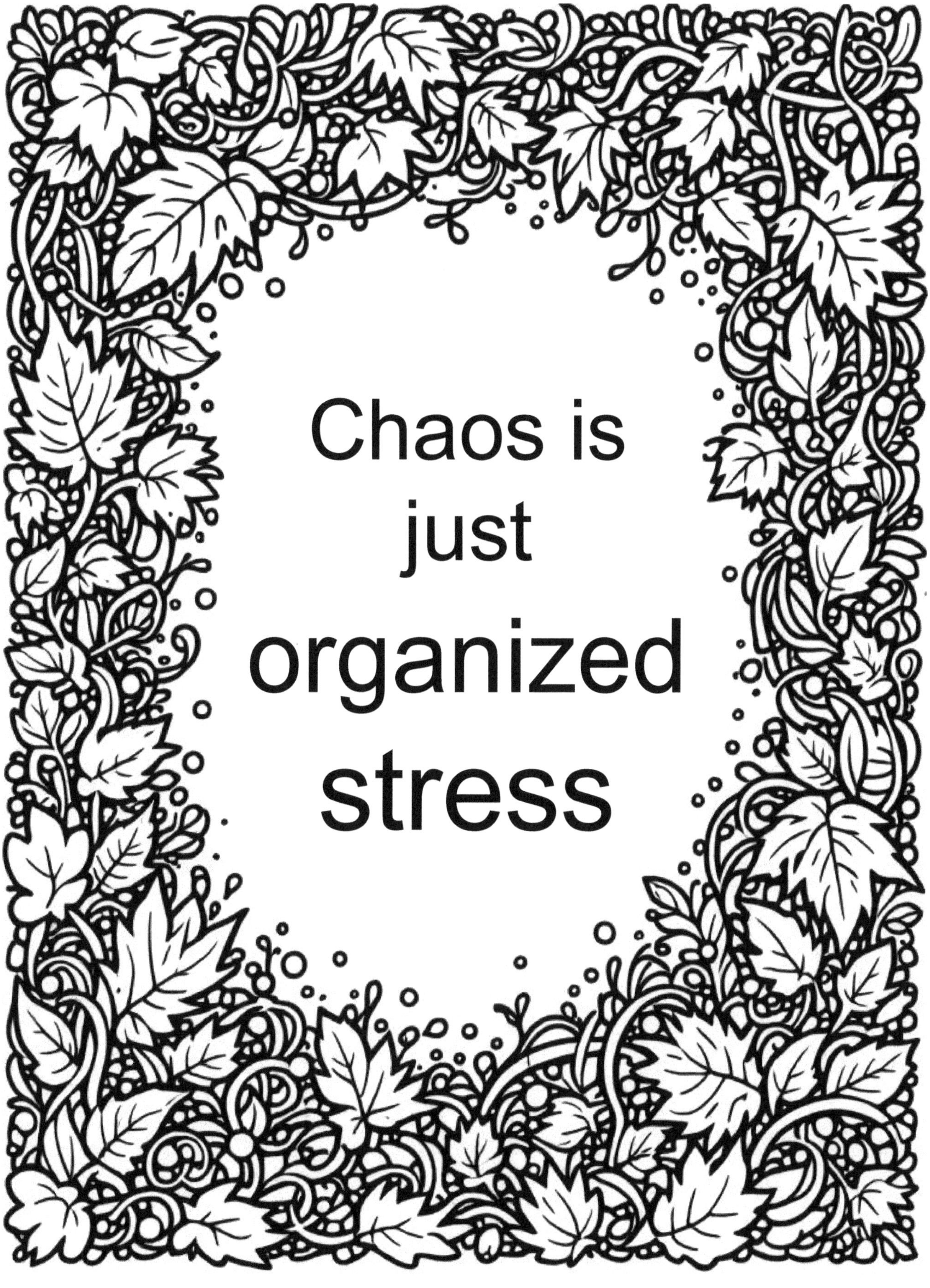
Chaos is
just
organized
stress

The next day, fueled by her newfound determination (and three cups of coffee), Lily resolves to reclaim control of her life.

She makes a to-do list titled *"Operation Adulting"* with bullet points like:
- Clean the disaster zone (aka her apartment).
- Meal prep (or at least stop eating cereal for dinner).
- Actually open the mail that's been piling up for weeks.

She tackles the first item by starting with the dishes. Mid-scrub, she hears a suspicious *drip... drip...* from the ceiling. A water leak. "Of course," she mutters. "Why not add plumbing to my résumé?"

She calls the landlord, who promises to "send someone right over," which in landlord time means *never*. As she waits, Lily discovers the mail pile includes three overdue bills and a jury summons. "Adulting is my passion," she whispers sarcastically, fighting back tears.

Continue on p56

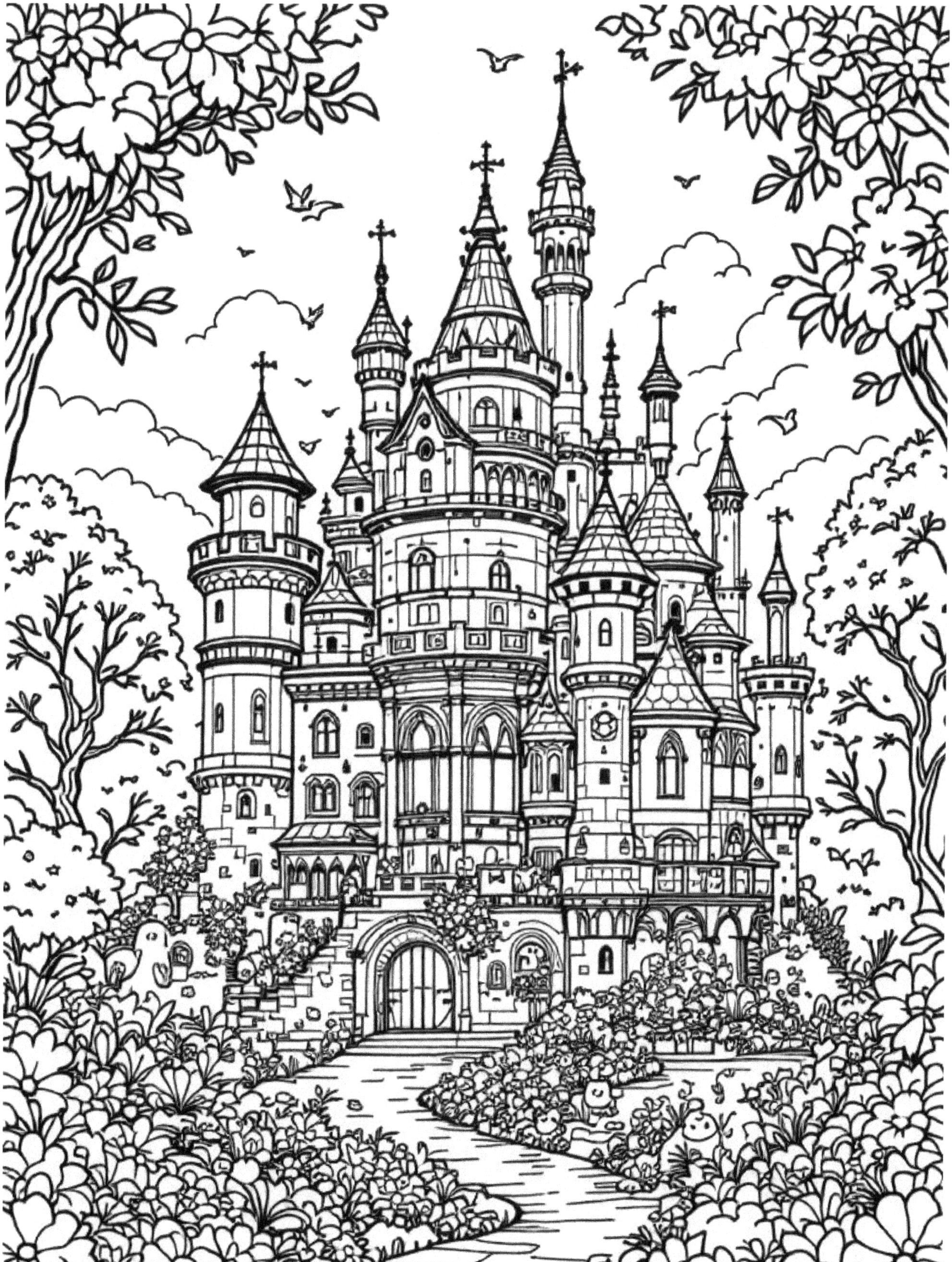

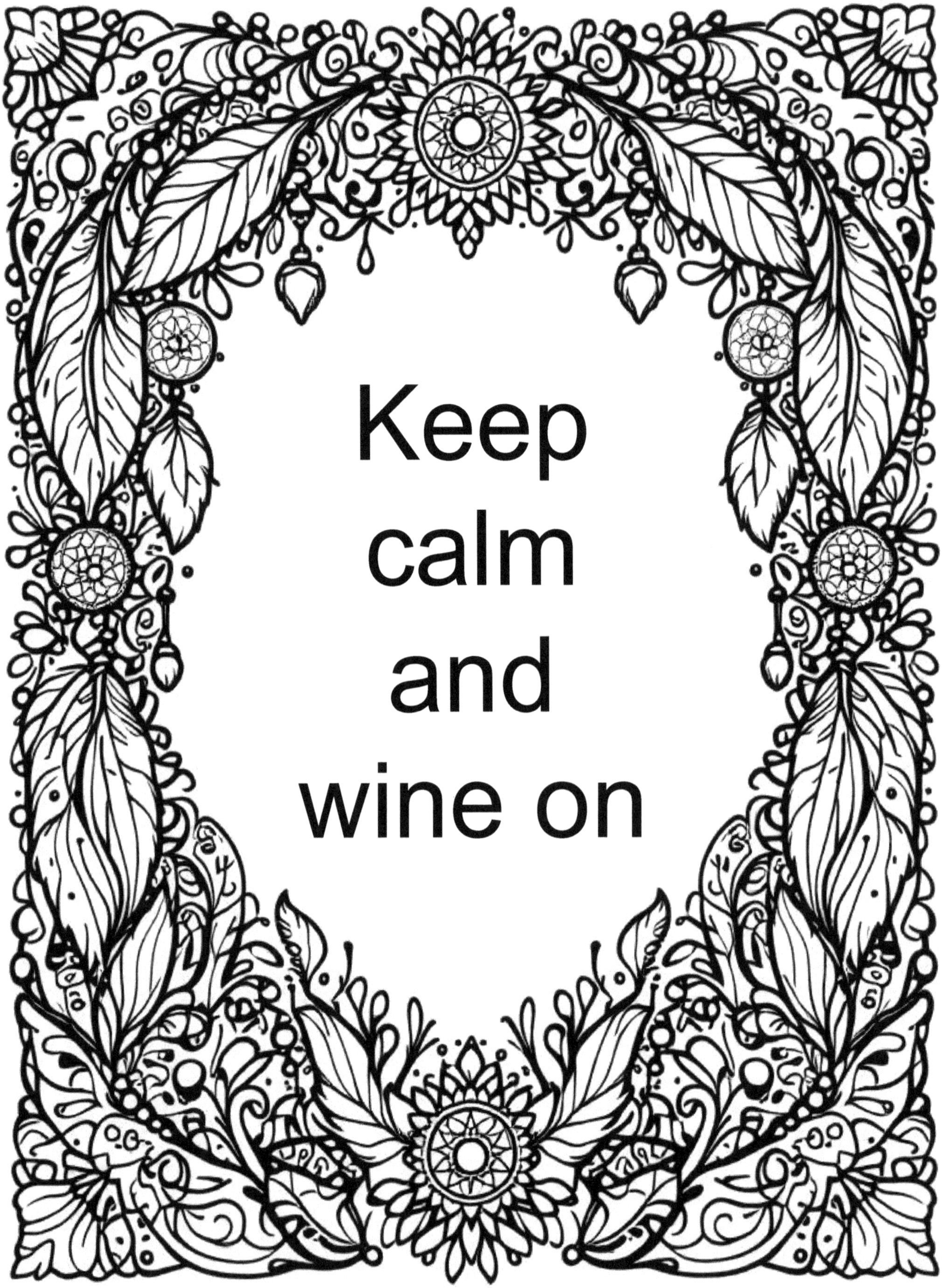
Keep
calm
and
wine on

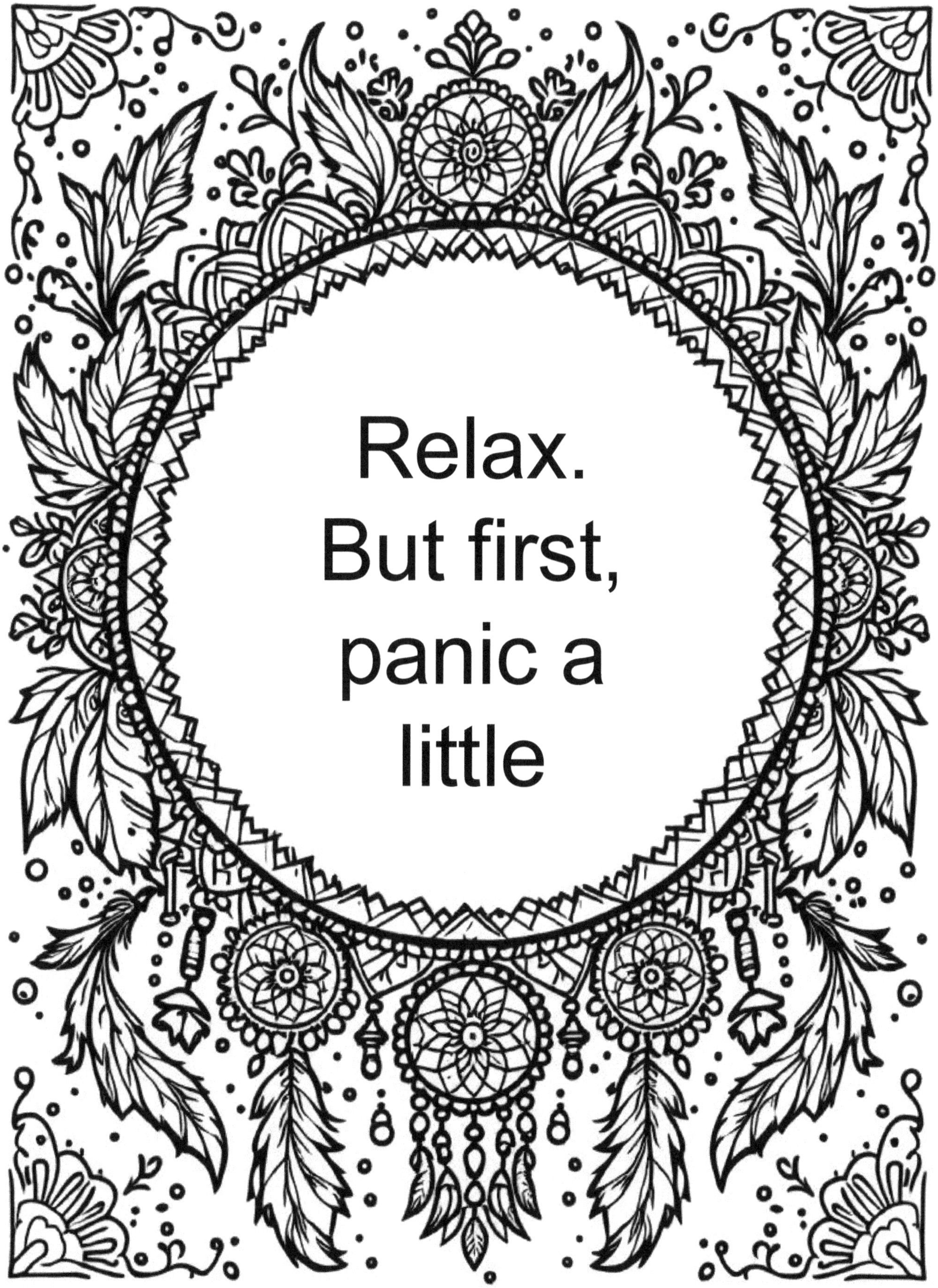
Relax.
But first,
panic a
little

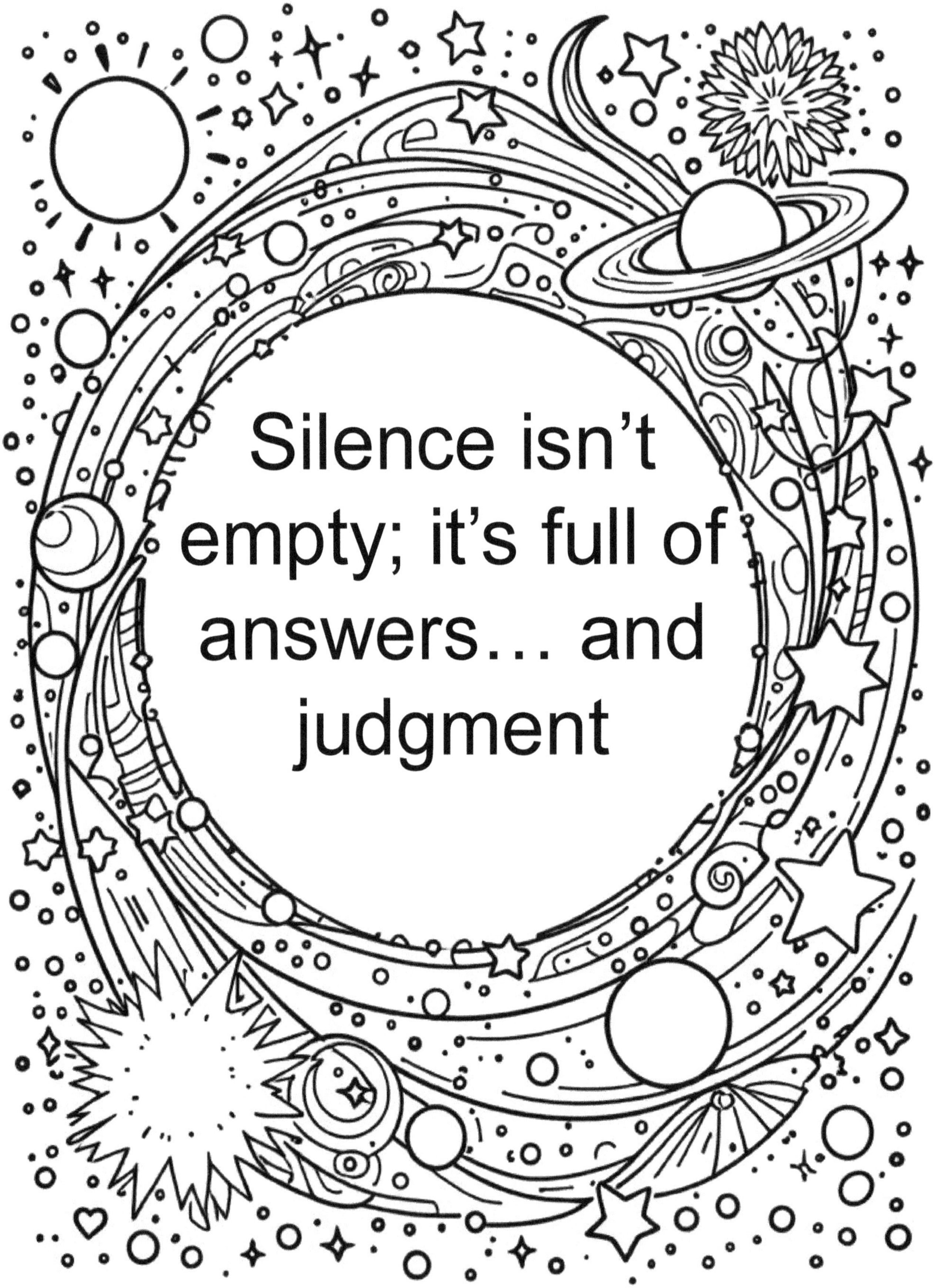
Silence isn't
empty; it's full of
answers… and
judgment

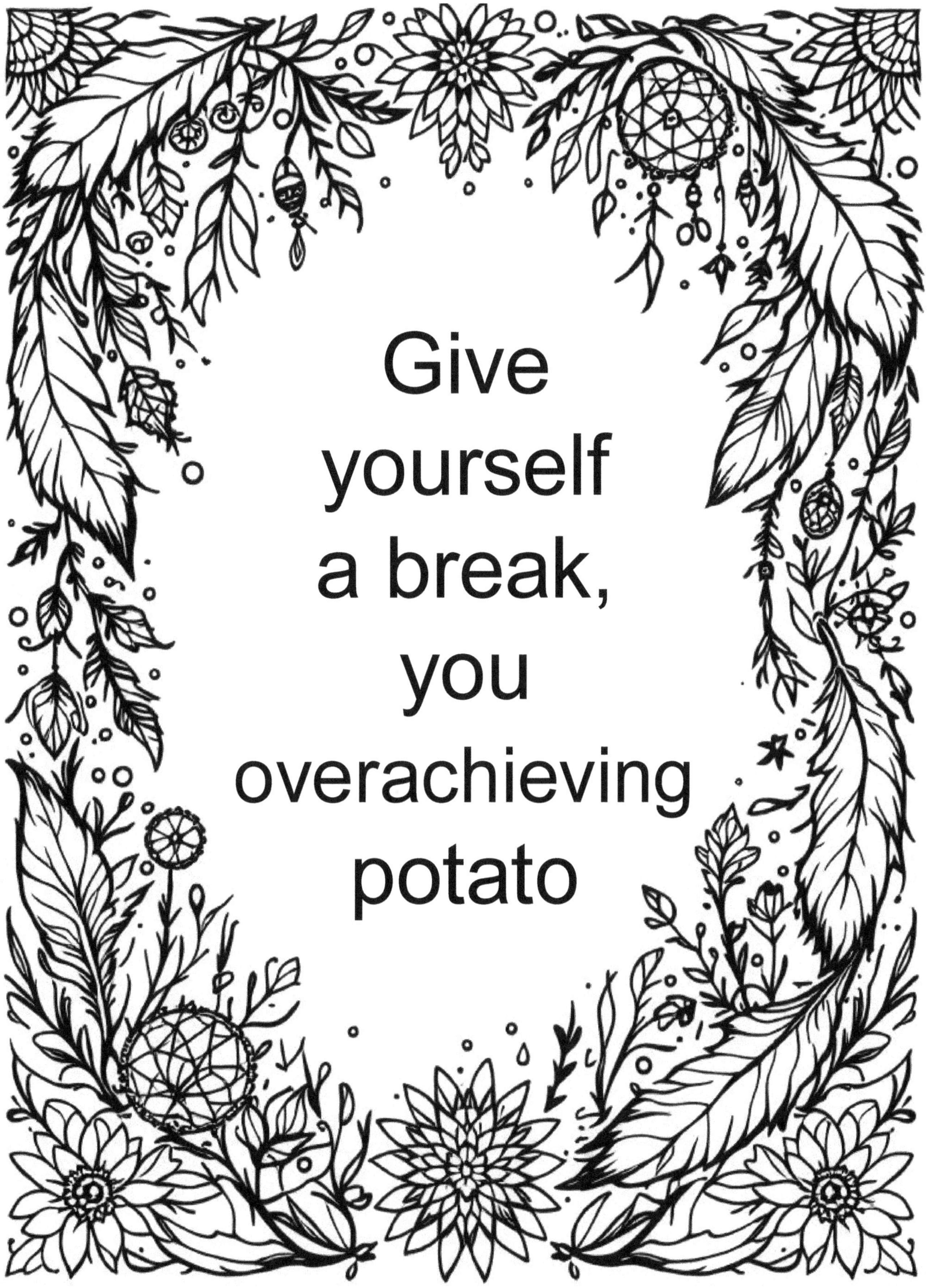
Give
yourself
a break,
you
overachieving
potato

Take life
one
meltdown
at
a time

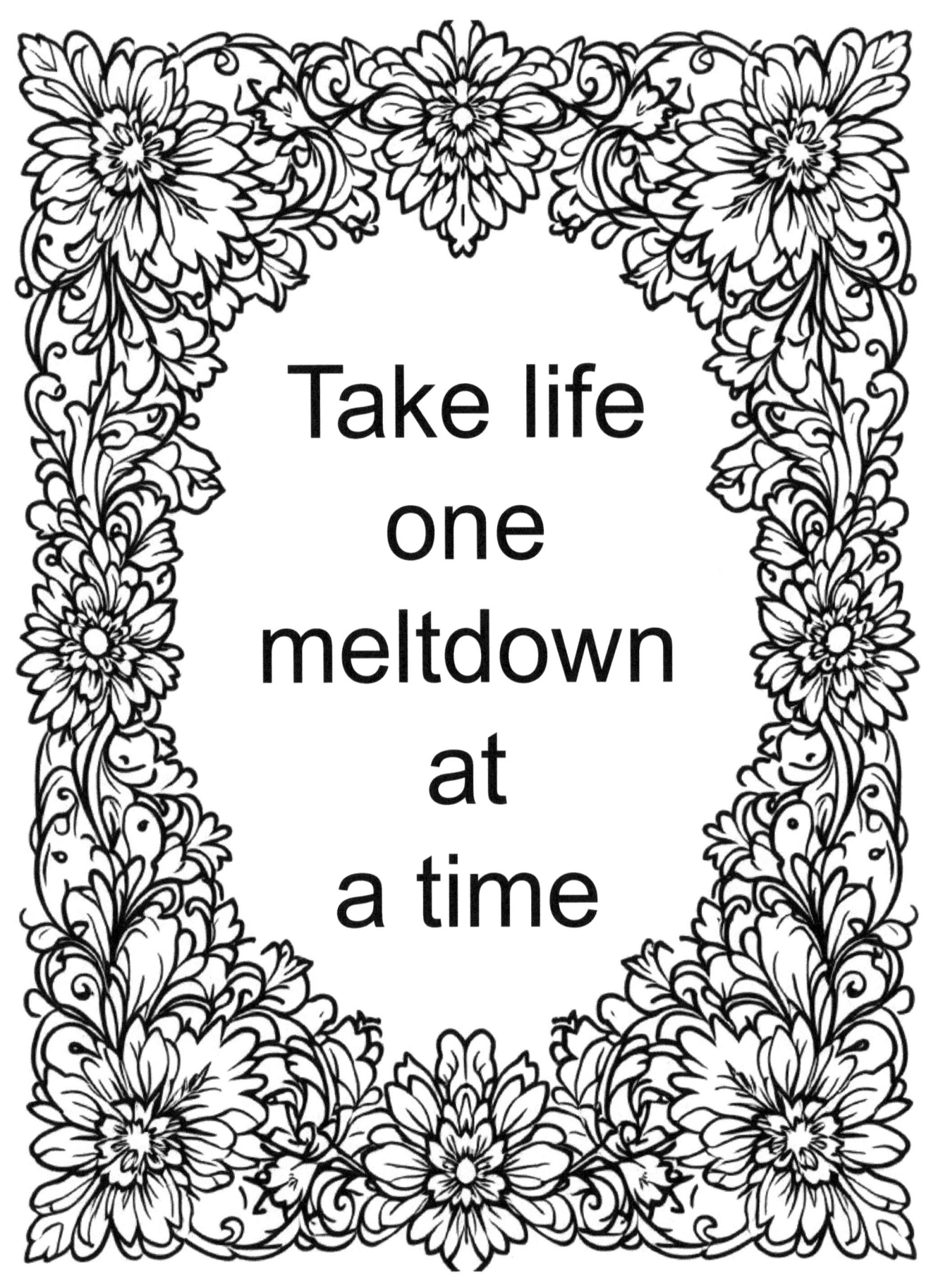

If at first you don’t succeed, take a nap

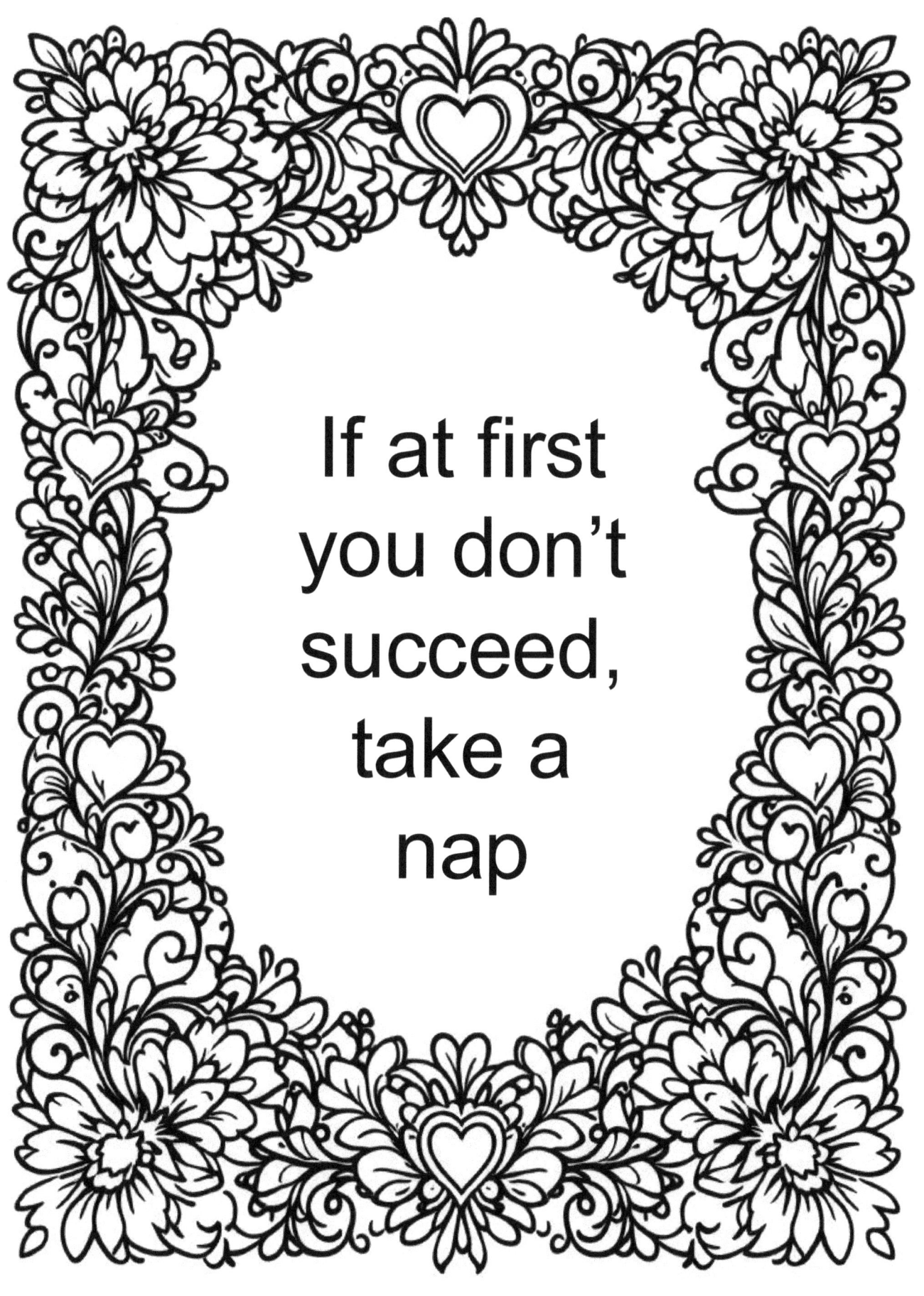

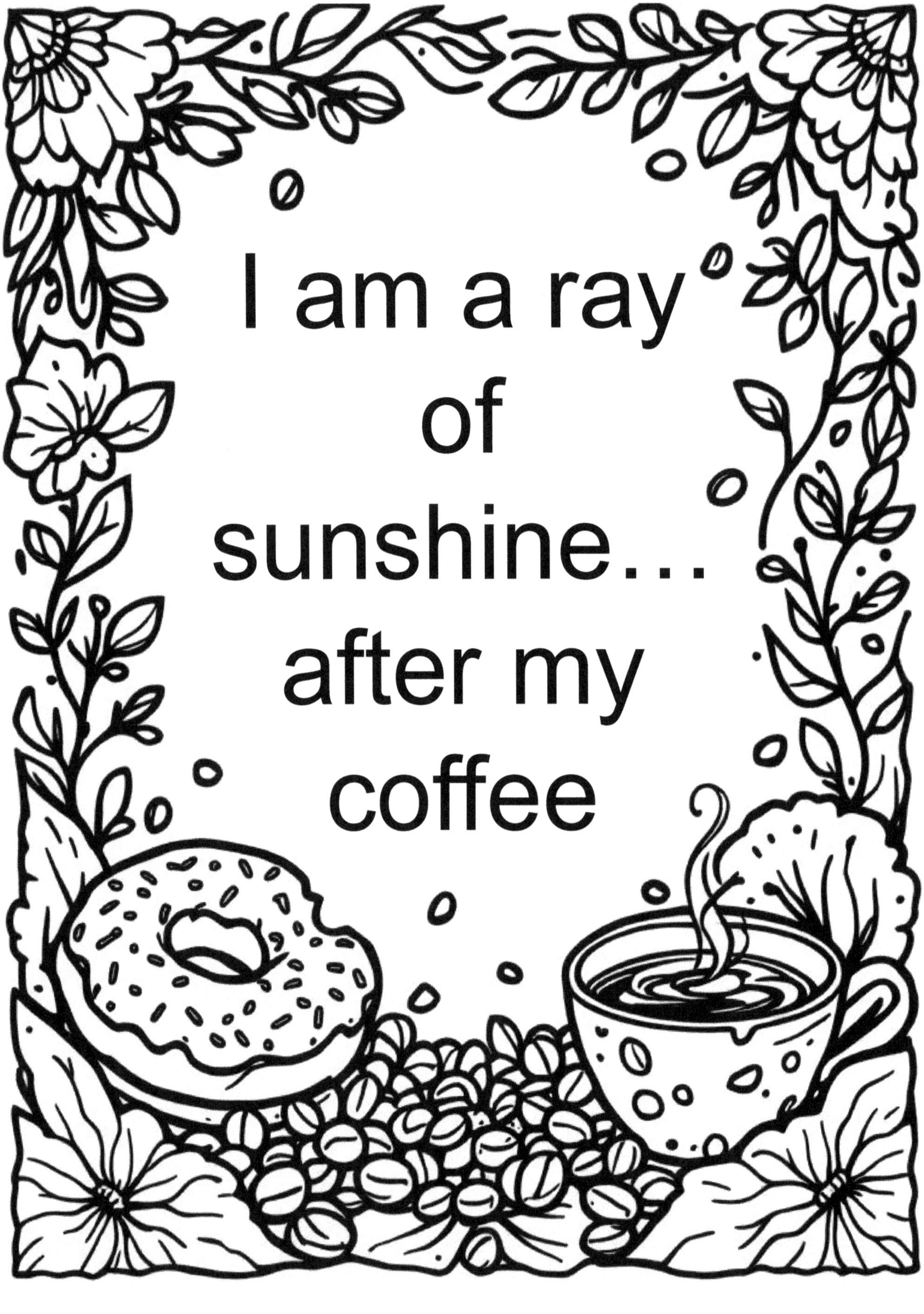
I am a ray
of
sunshine…
after my
coffee

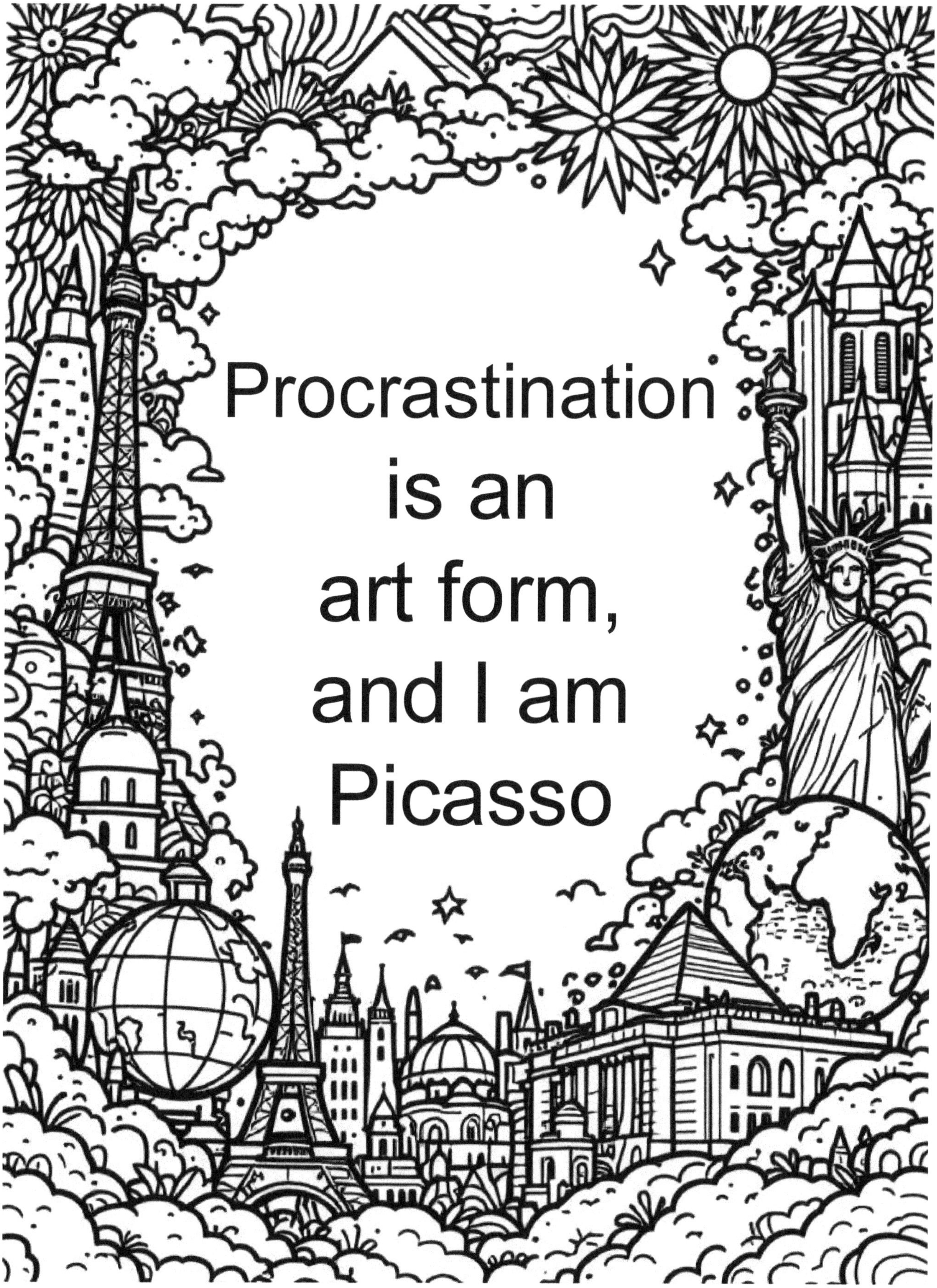
Procrastination
is an
art form,
and I am
Picasso

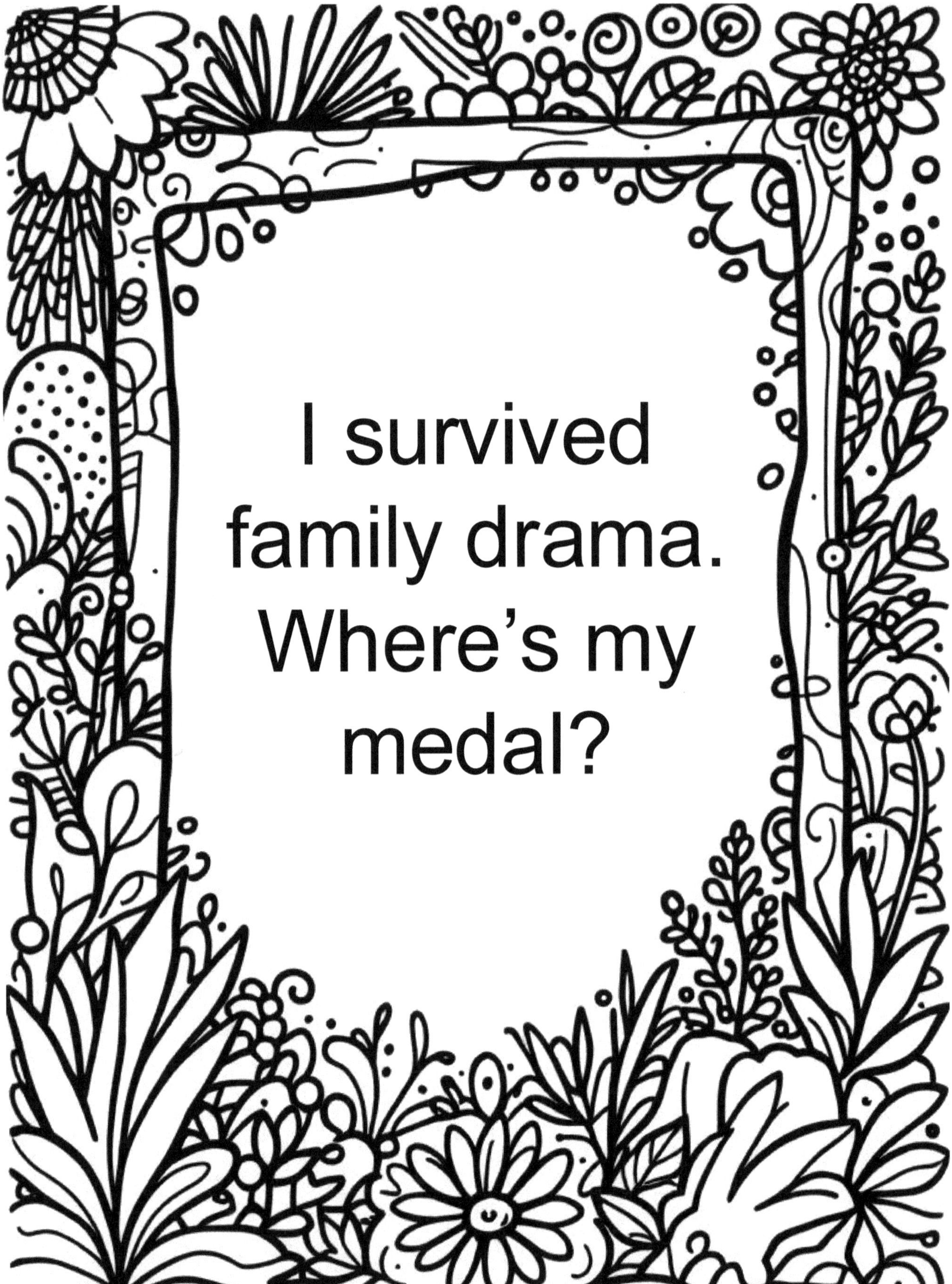
I survived family drama. Where's my medal?

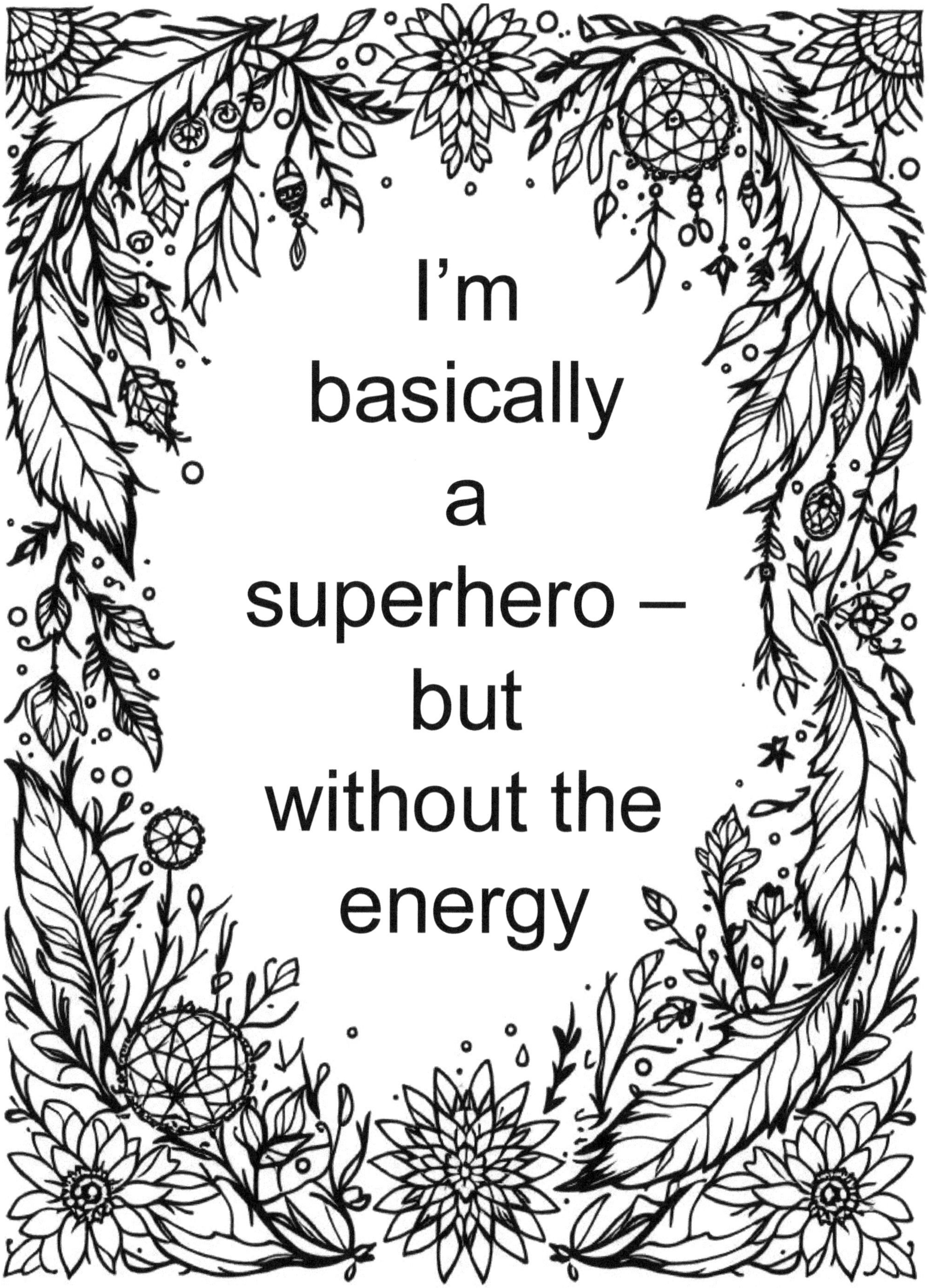

I’m
basically
a
superhero –
but
without the
energy

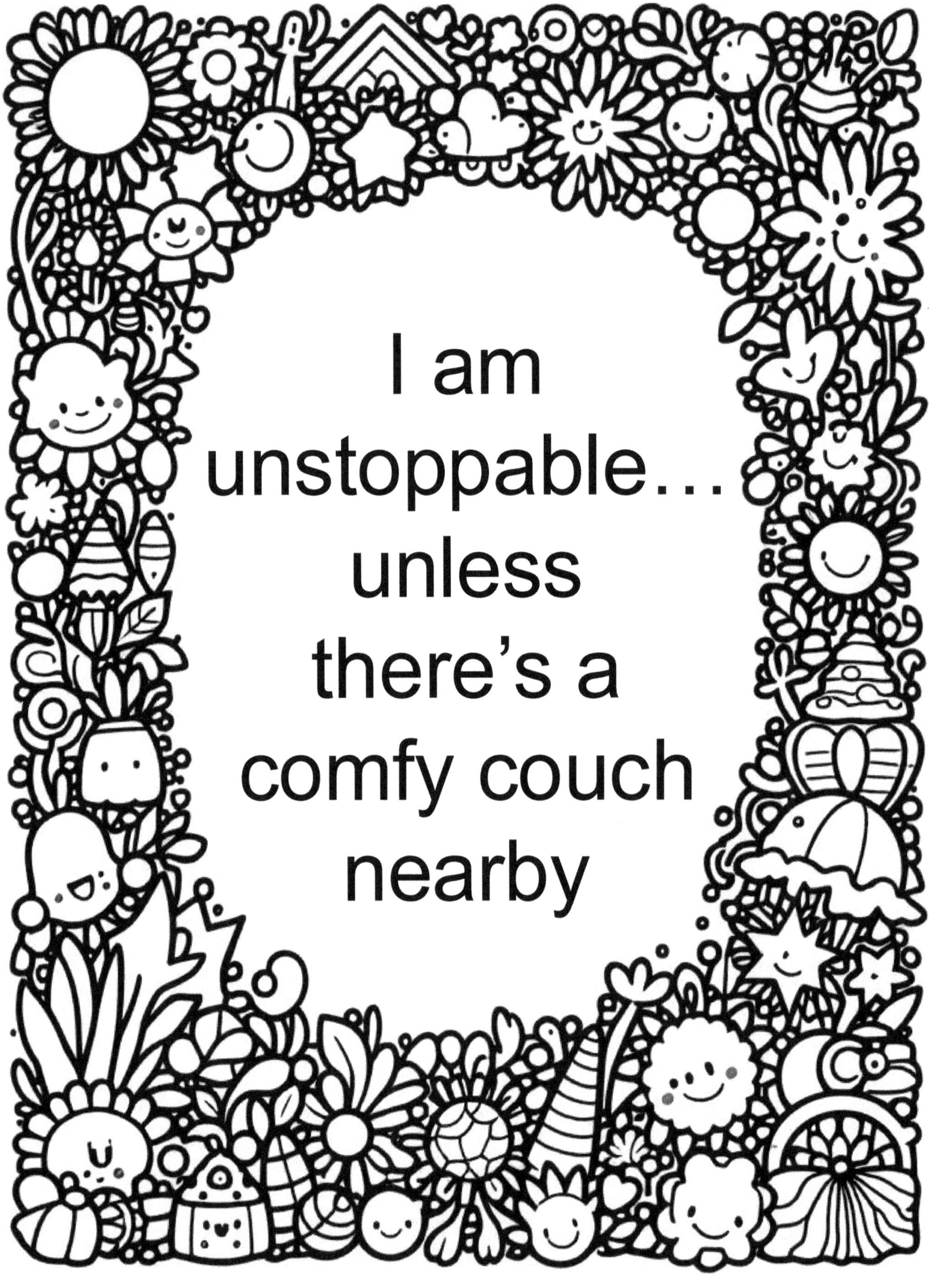

I am unstoppable… unless there’s a comfy couch nearby

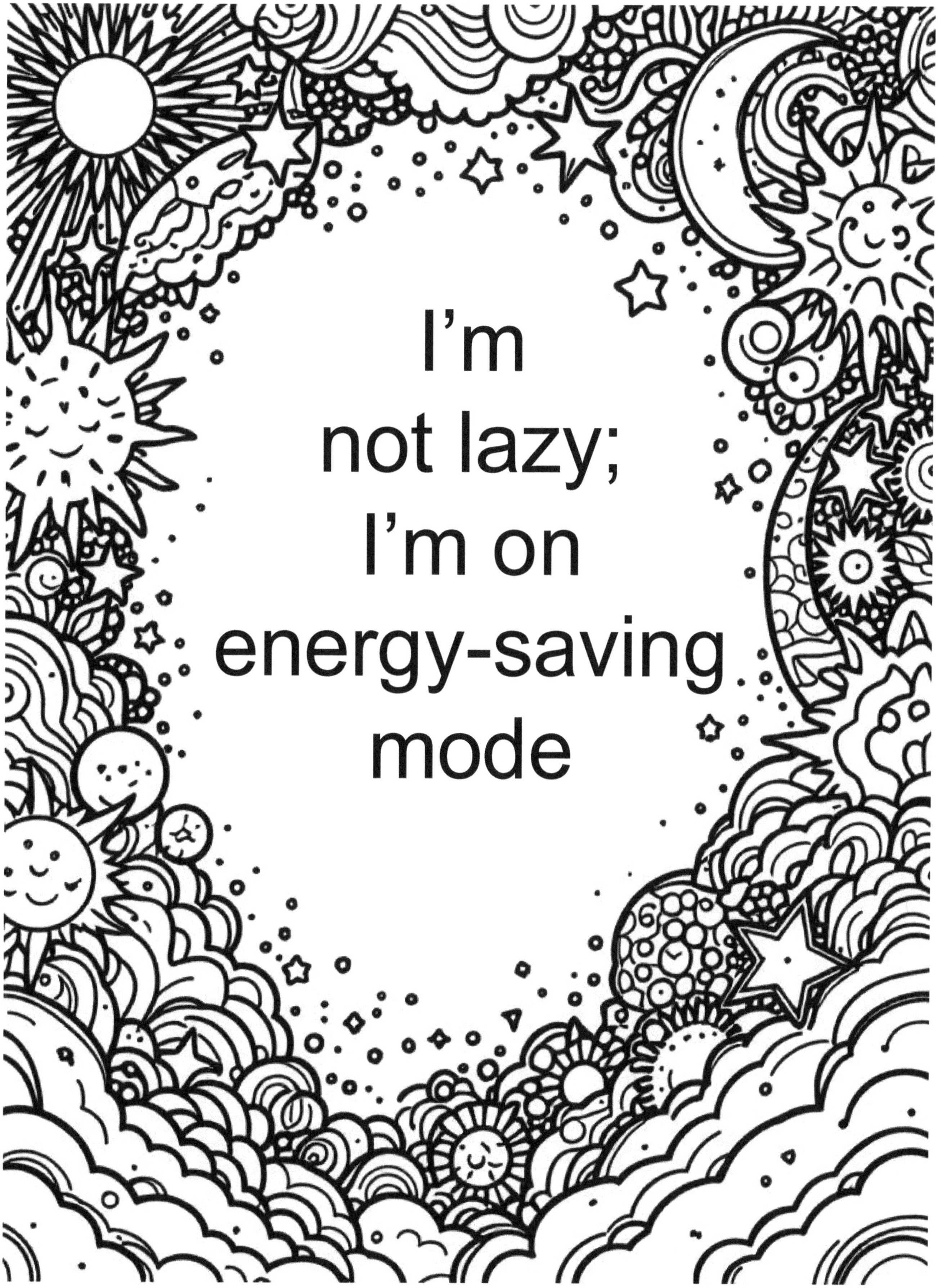
I'm
not lazy;
I'm on
energy-saving
mode

By Friday, Lily is at her wit's end. Her zen experiment has spiraled into a week of chaos. She's ready to give up when her best friend, Mia, suggests a girls' night out. "Hakuna Moscato," Mia says, handing Lily a wine glass. "It means no worries."

Over appetizers, Lily confesses her plan to "reset her life" starting January 1. Mia laughs. "Oh, you mean New Year's resolutions? You've tried that every year since college."

"This time will be different," Lily insists, swirling her wine. "I'll finally become one of those people who drinks green juice, meditates daily, and wakes up at 5 a.m."

Mia raises an eyebrow. "Or, hear me out… you could just embrace the chaos."

Before Lily can argue, her phone buzzes with a calendar reminder: *"Annual Resolution Planning Meeting: Dec 31, 11:59 PM."* She groans. "Why do I do this to myself?"

As the night winds down, Lily stares at her reflection in the bar's bathroom mirror. "I've got this," she says, psyching herself up. "Next year will be my year." But deep down, she knows the chaos isn't going anywhere.

* * *

On New Year's Eve, Lily is furiously scribbling resolutions on the back of a napkin. Just as the clock strikes midnight, fireworks explode outside—and the sprinkler system inside… Soaked and defeated, she mutters, "the new year is already off to a great start."

TO BE CONTINUED IN: "New Year Resolutions Gone Wrong."

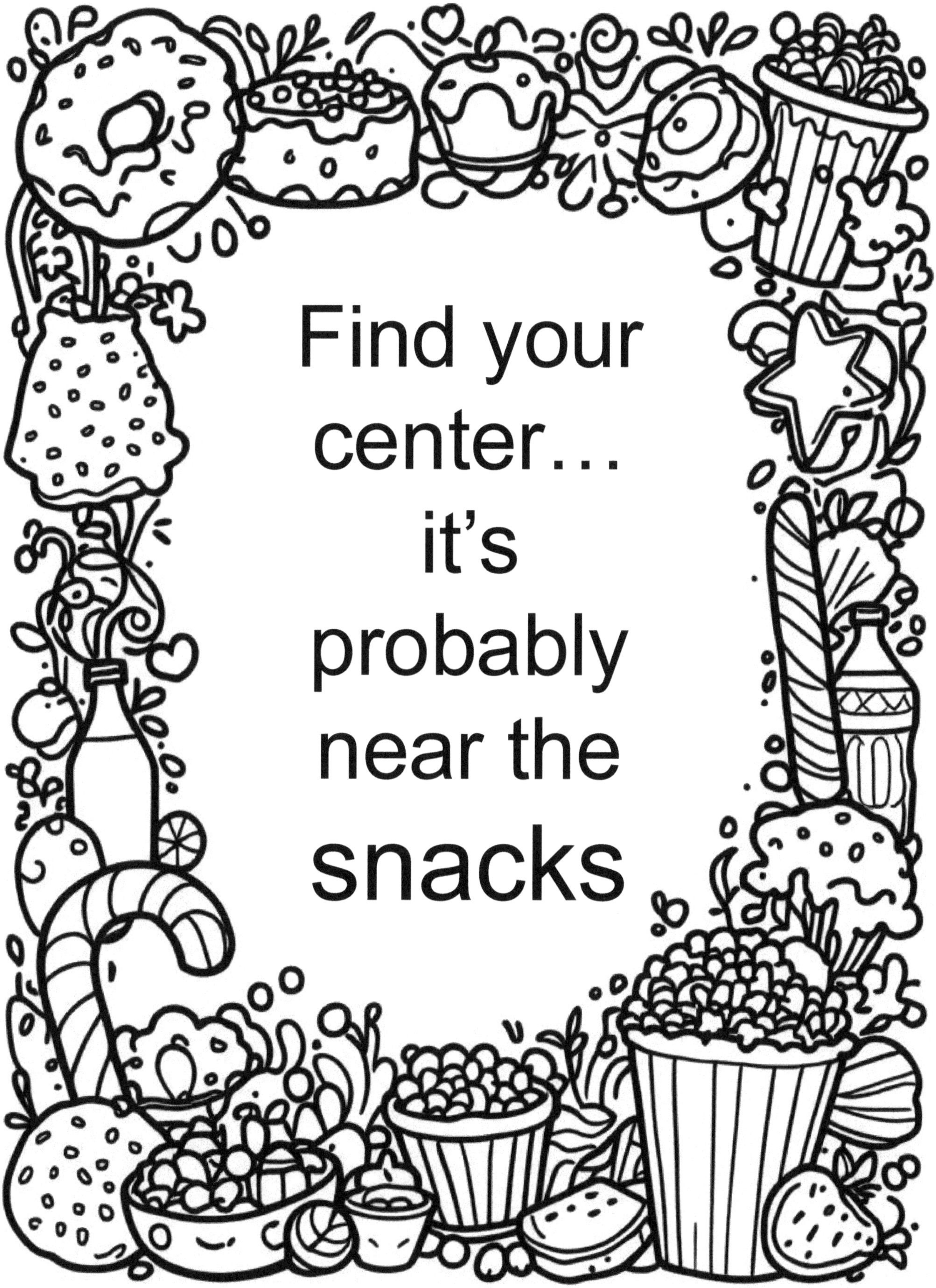

Find your center… it's probably near the snacks

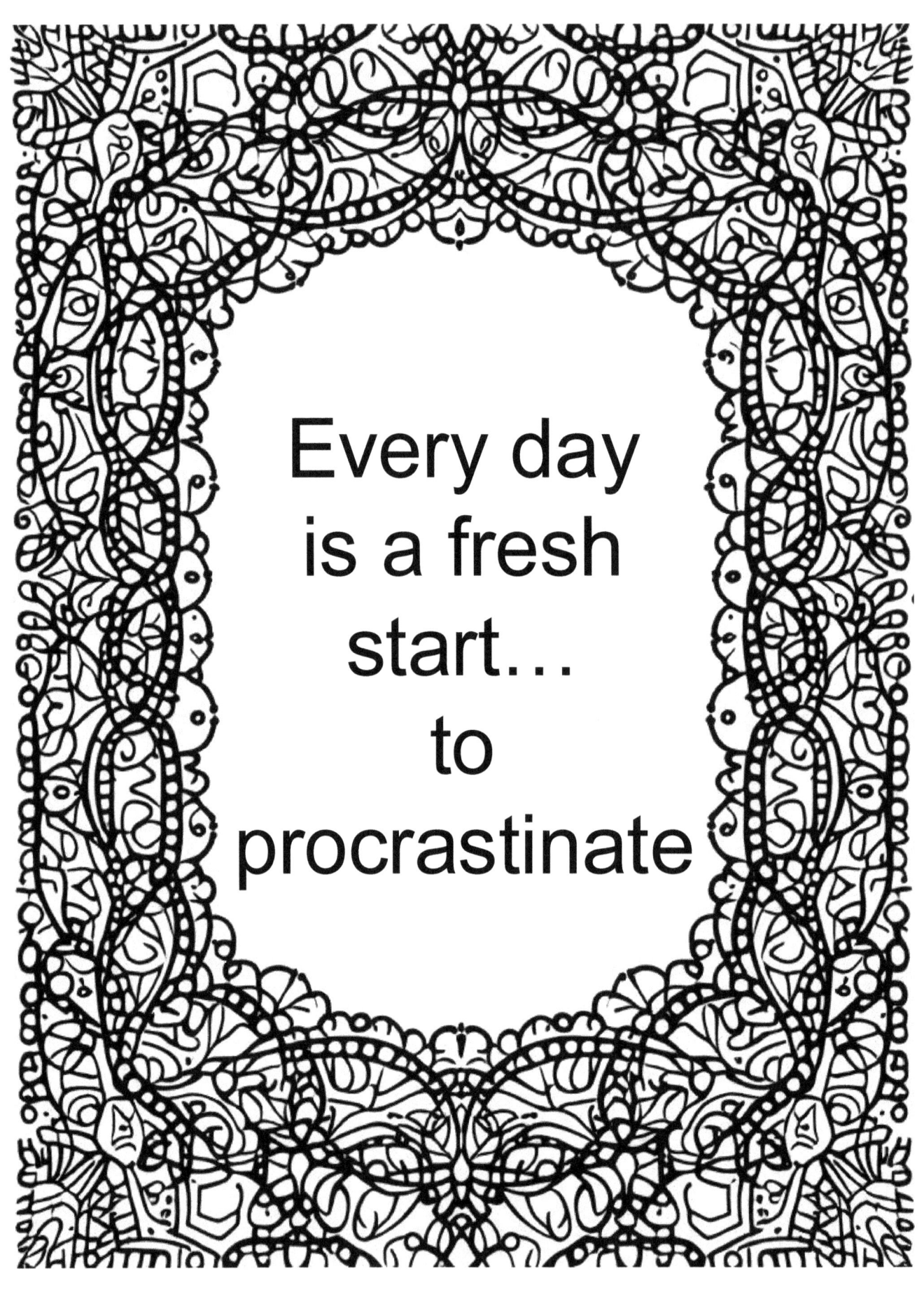
Every day is a fresh start… to procrastinate

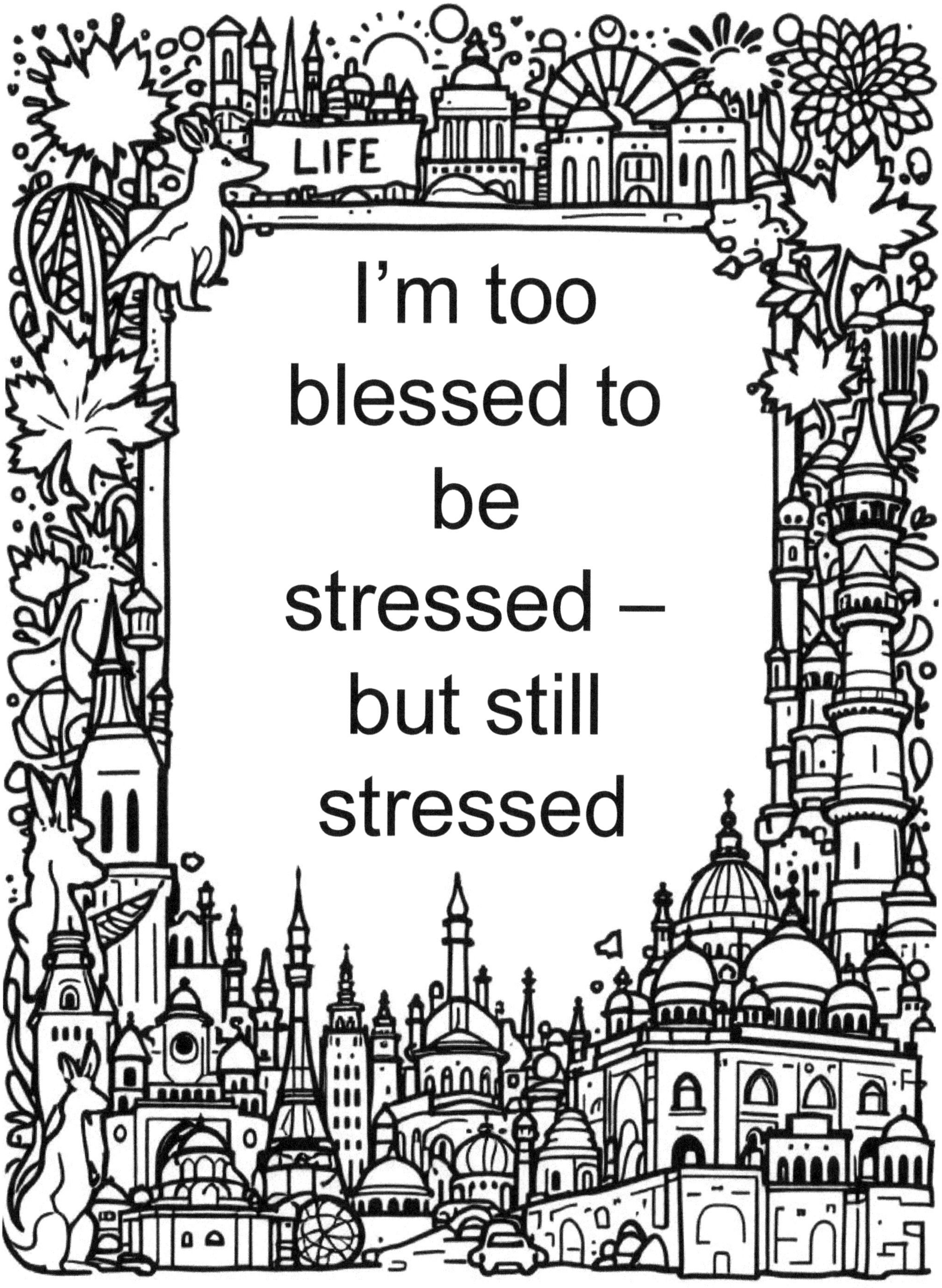
LIFE

I’m too blessed to be stressed – but still stressed

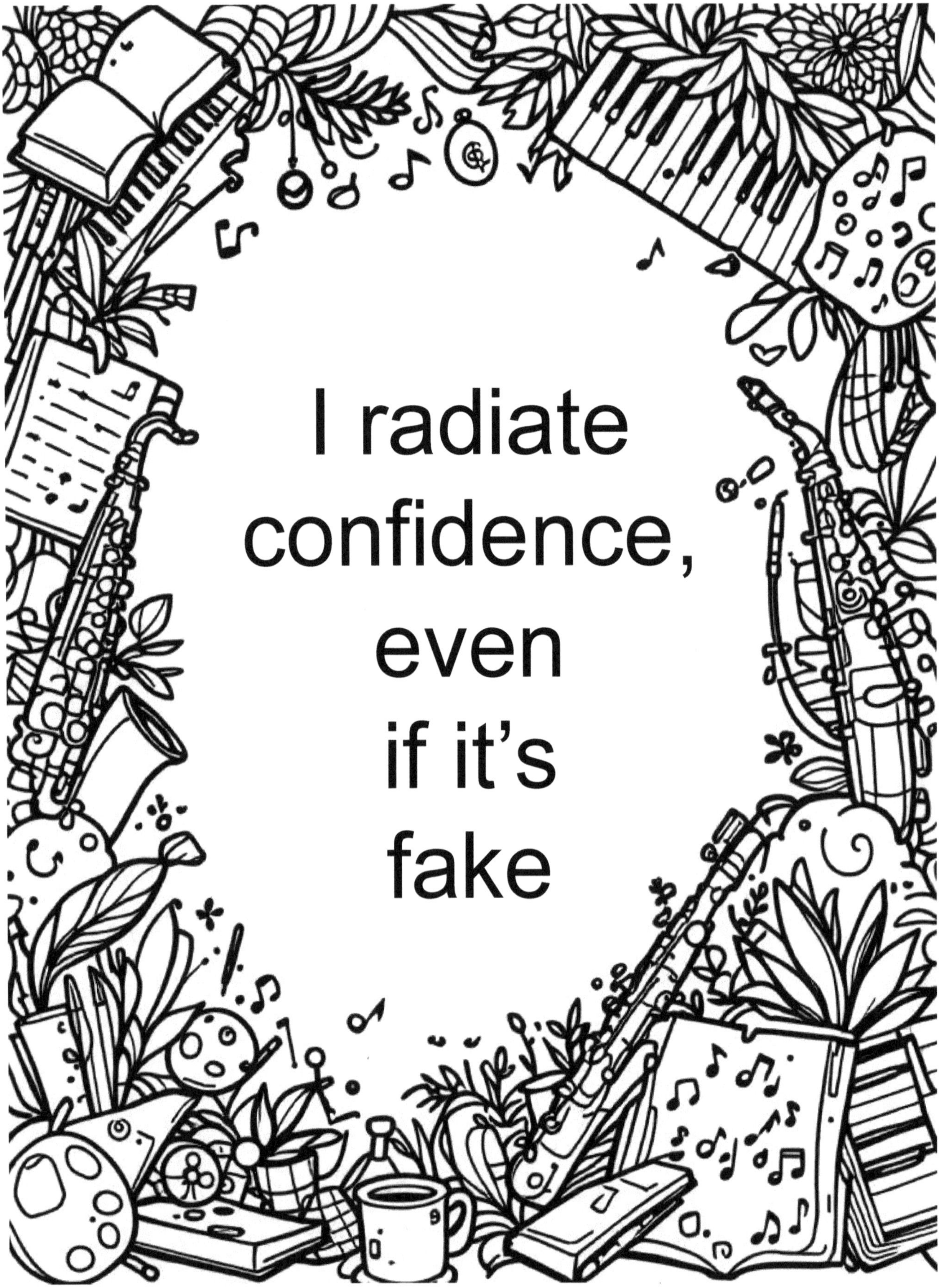

I radiate
confidence,
even
if it’s
fake

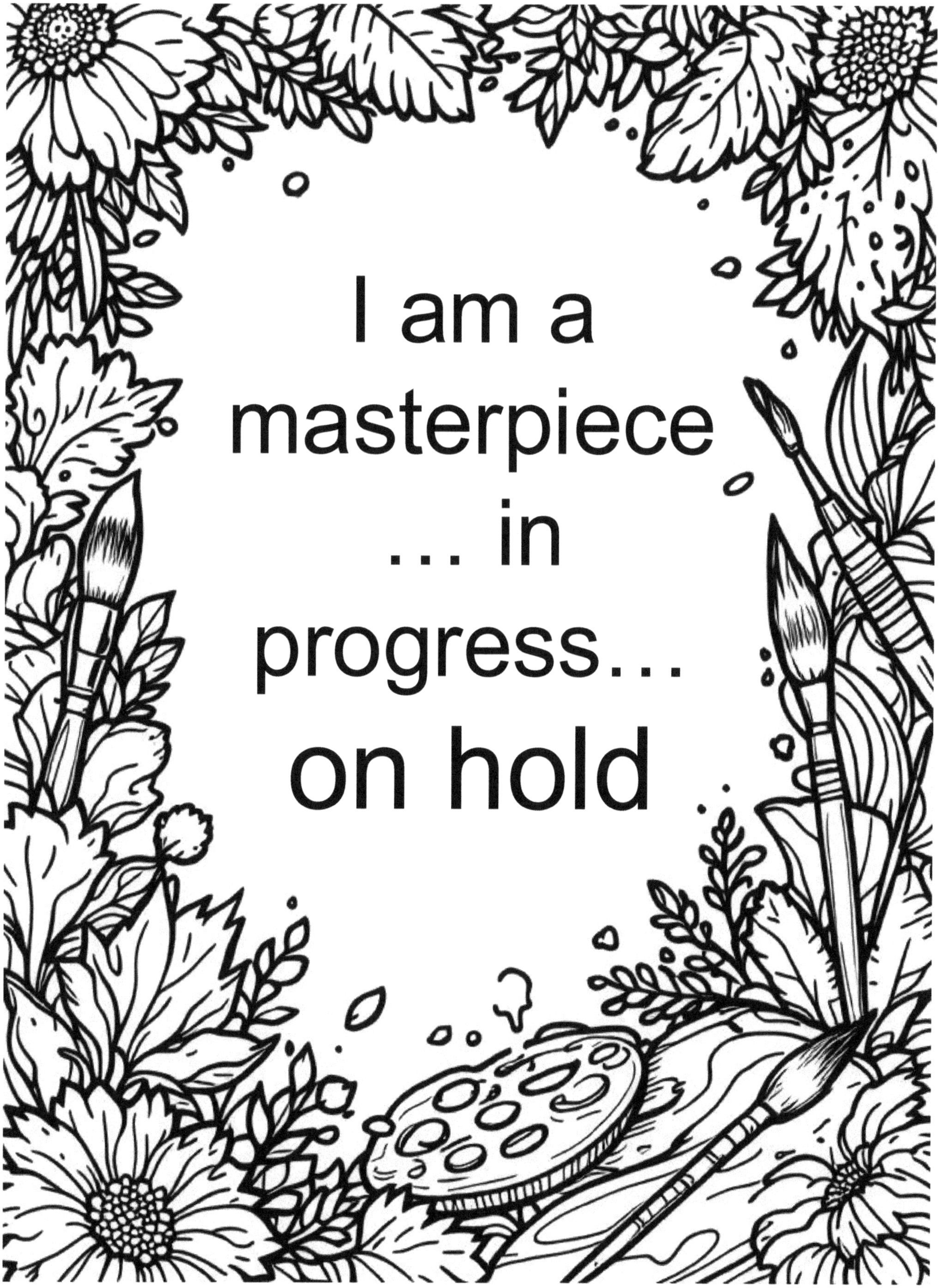
I am a
masterpiece
… in
progress…
on hold

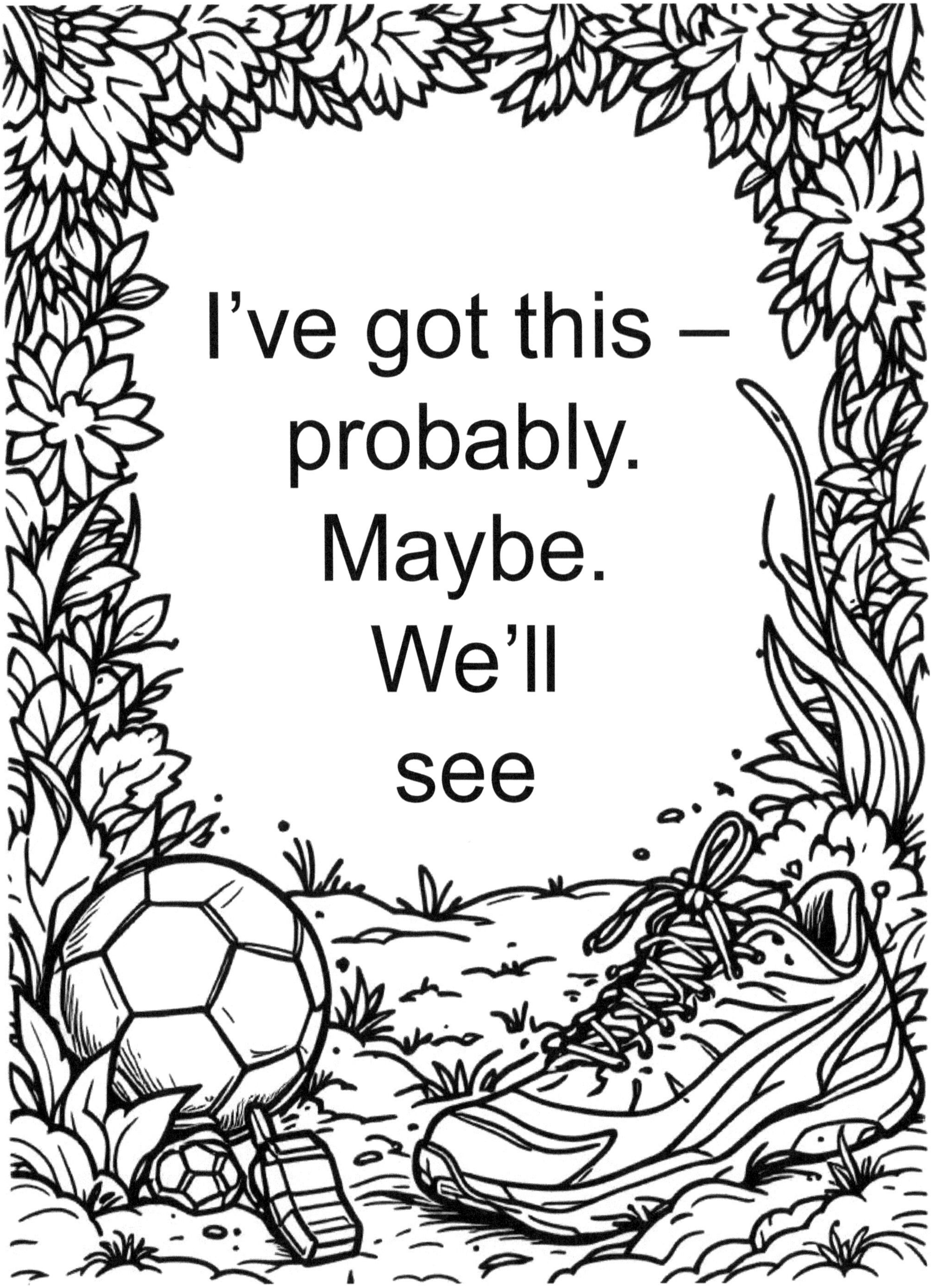
I’ve got this – probably. Maybe. We’ll see

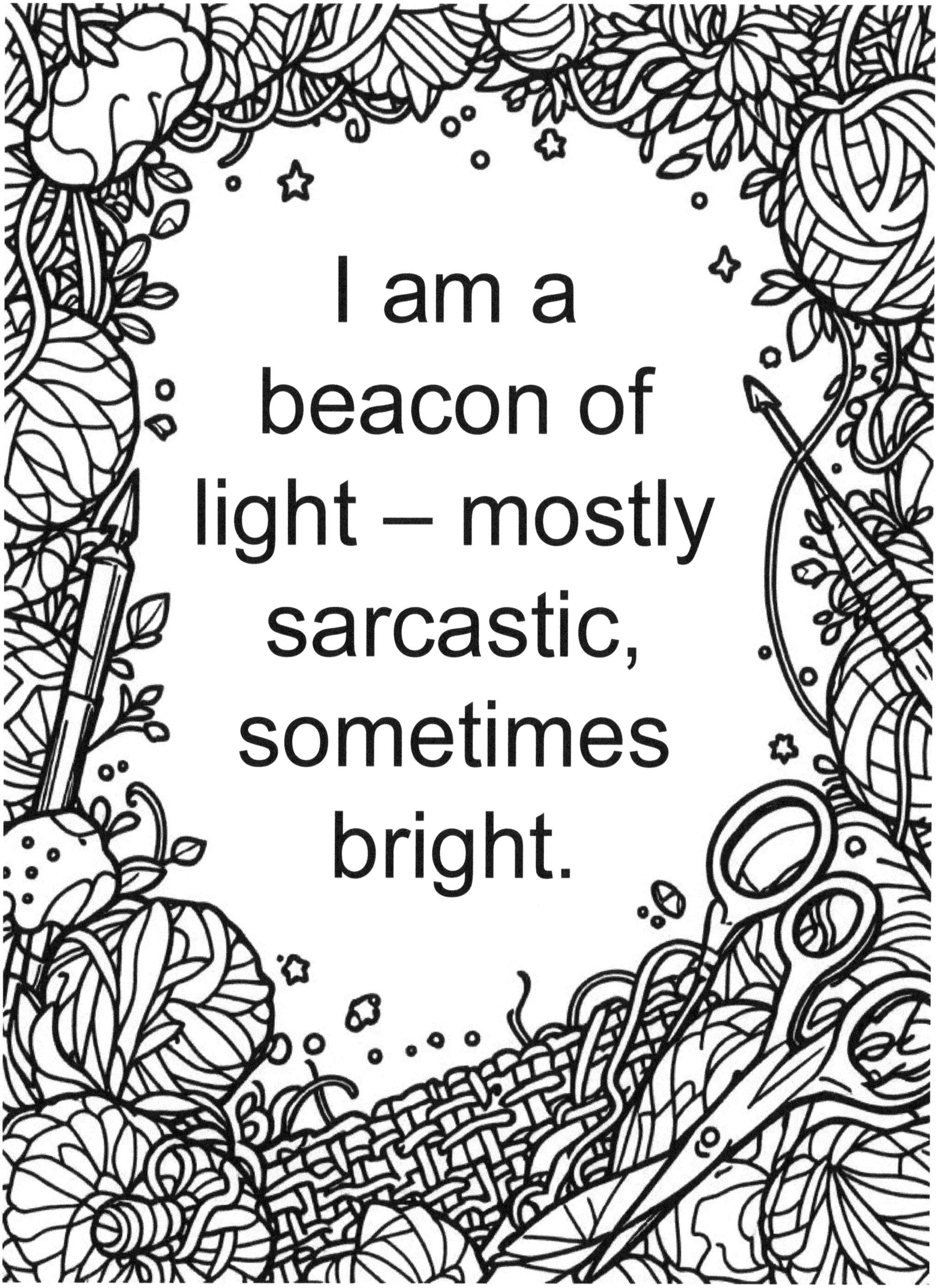

I am a
beacon of
light – mostly
sarcastic,
sometimes
bright.

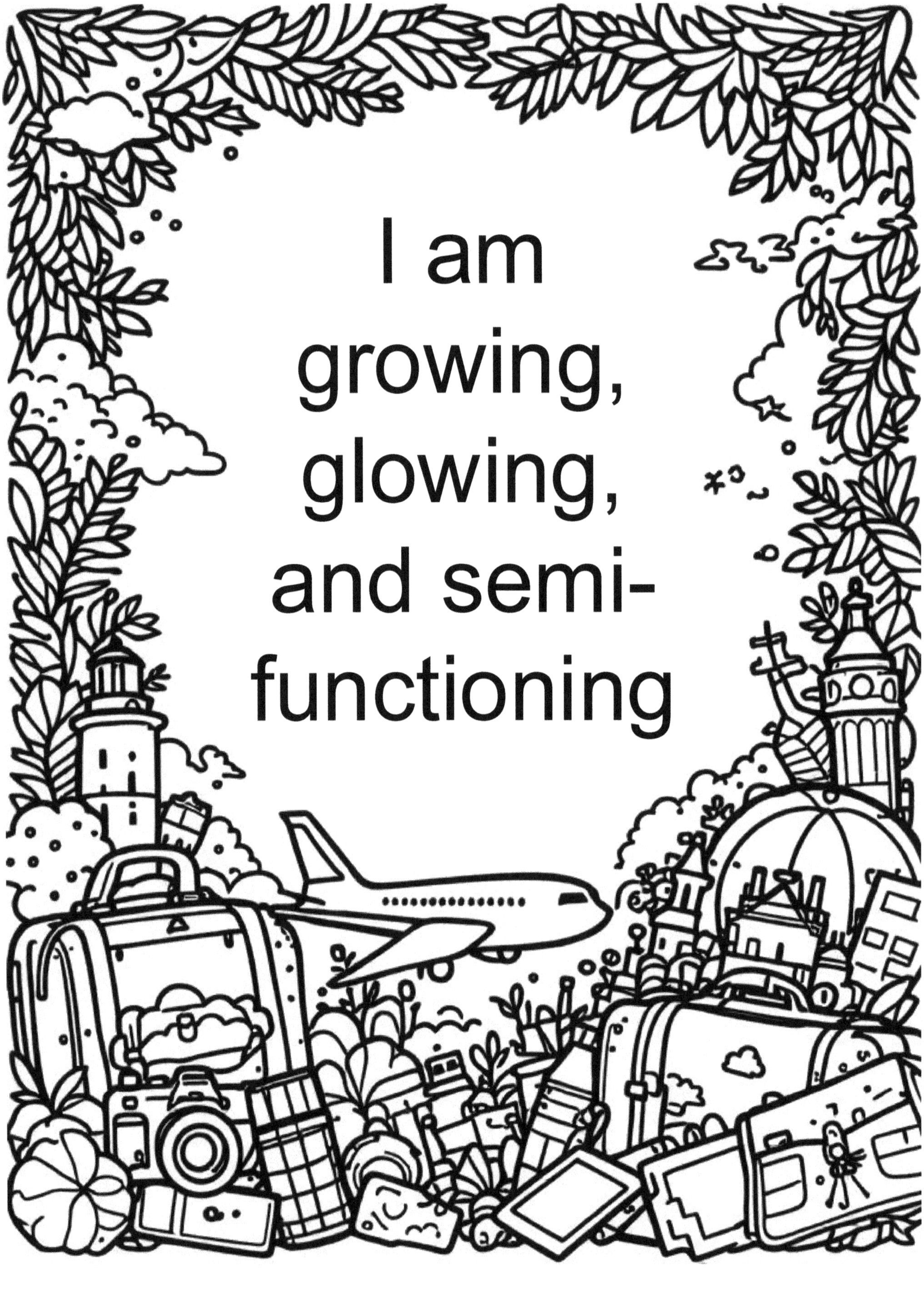
I am
growing,
glowing,
and semi-
functioning

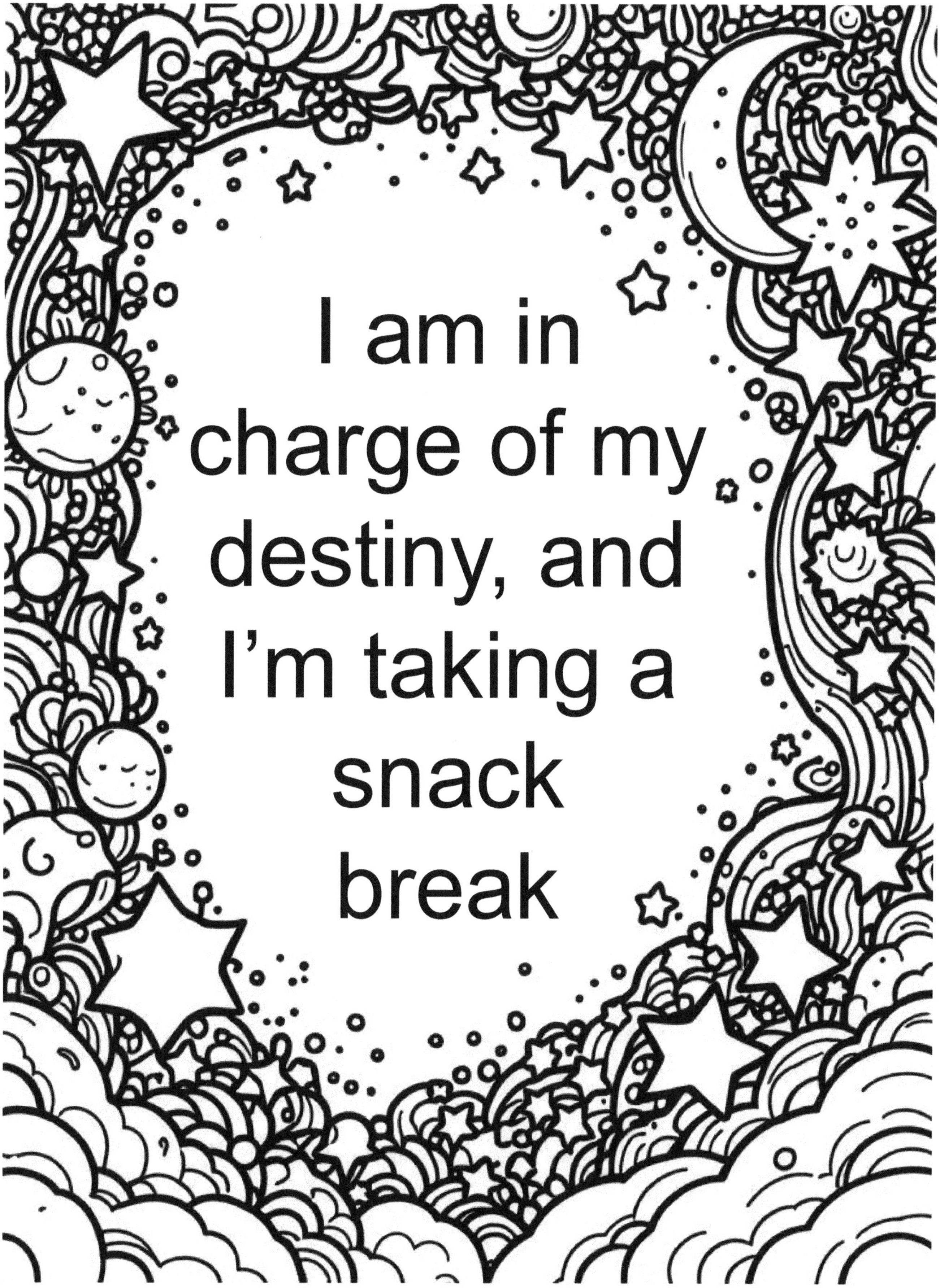
I am in
charge of my
destiny, and
I'm taking a
snack
break

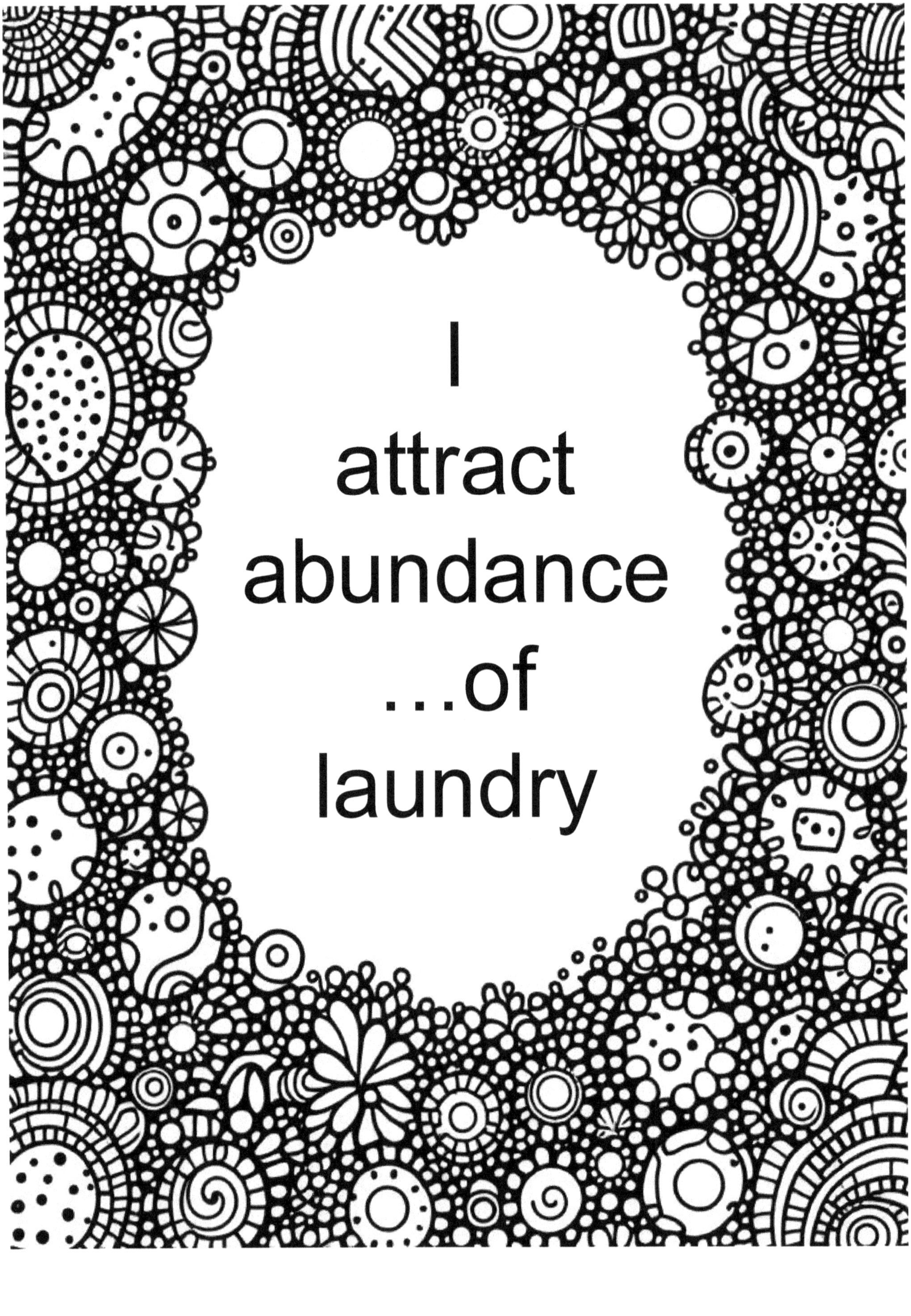

I
attract
abundance
...of
laundry

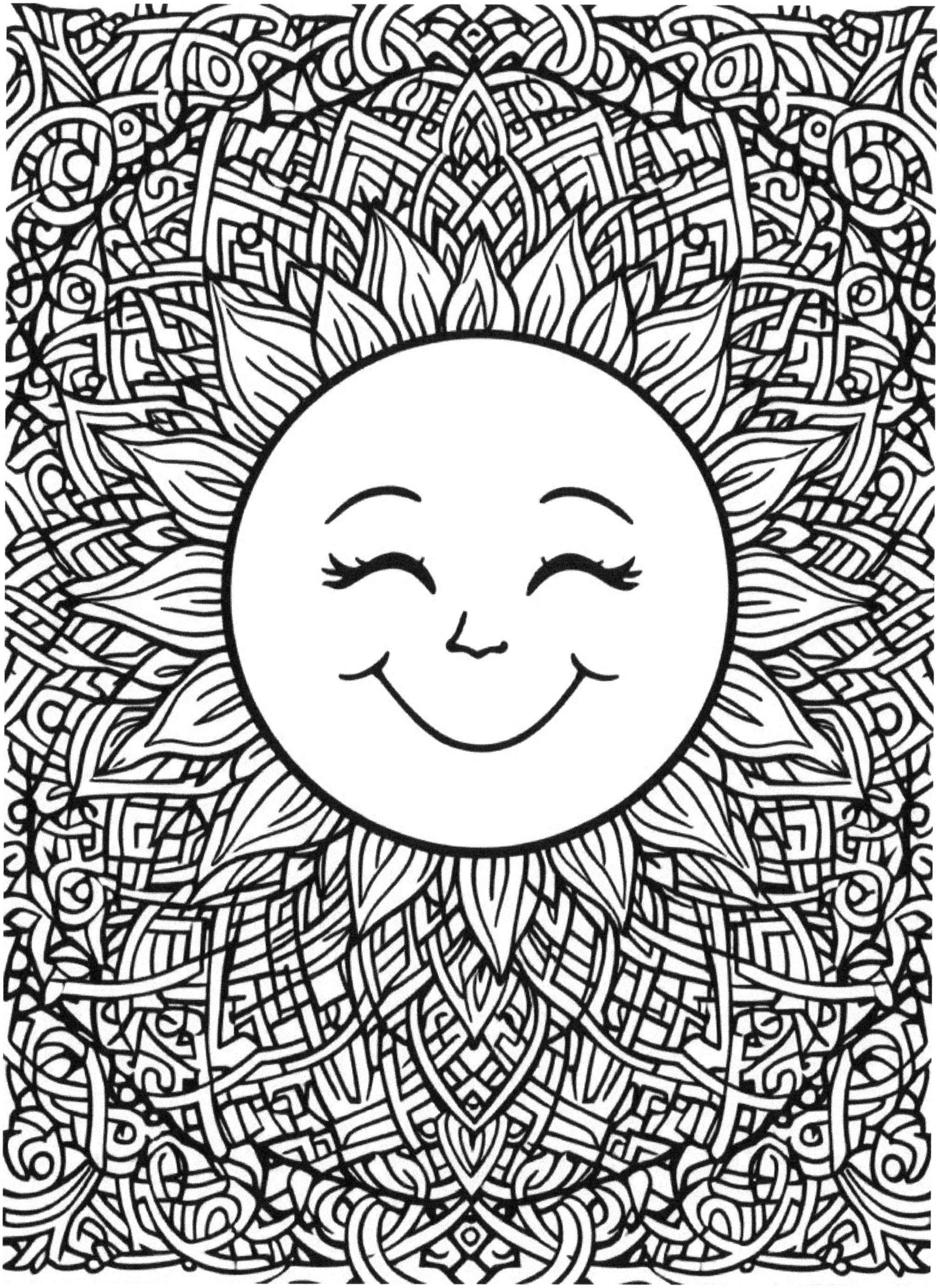

www.ingramcontent.com/pod-product-compliance
Lightning Source LLC
LaVergne TN
LVHW070217080526
838202LV00067B/6840